"This gorgeous book is a celebration of wild food, foraging, and cultivating connection to the natural world. The recipes inside highlight ingredients from coast to forest and inspire you to get creative, get outside, and participate in the surrounding ecosystem; to live a healthier, more pleasurable, and more delicious life."

—**EMMA TEAL PRIVAT AND CLAIRE NEATON**, co-owners of Salmon Sisters and authors of *The Salmon Sisters: Feasting, Fishing, and Living in Alaska*

"A deliciously thoughtful book with plenty of recipes for beginning or experienced foragers. I'll have the mushroom pâté, cheesy pasta with truffles, and a candy cap old-fashioned, please."

—**ALAN BERGO**, James Beard Award–winning chef and author, and winner of Hulu's *Chefs vs. Wild*

"Steeped in the magic of the West Coast, *Forage. Gather. Feast.* is a beautiful book. Maria's deeply intuitive approach to cooking celebrates an abundance of wild foods from seaside to forests. Her book will be favorite in my kitchen for a long time."

—**JENNY MCGRUTHER**, author of *The Nourished Kitchen* and *Vibrant Botanticals*

"Flaming Pine Needle Mussels! Stinging Nettle Gnocchi! Cherry Blossom Truffles! With her backwoods bona fides and visionary palate, Maria Finn has taken foraging to the next level. No matter where you live, *Forage. Gather. Feast.* will unlock the layers of meaning and deliciousness permeating our woods and coastlines. Your kitchen game will never be the same. Neither will your soul."

—**ROWAN JACOBSEN**, author of *Truffle Hound* and *A Geography of Oysters*

"Maria Finn draws you into a deeper connection to nature through its wonderful, wild foods. Food is the lure, but the end goal is a realignment of human systems in sync with the pace and beauty of Mother Nature."

—**BECKY SELENGUT**, author of *Good Fish* and *Shroom*

"Maria's recipes are both approachable and creative—from porcini and rosemary skewers and salt and lemon-preserved anchovies to seaweed butter, these recipes will inspire you to head for the woods, waterways, and urban green spaces—to forage, gather, and feast your way into a better life."

—**TIFFANY SHLAIN**, artist, author, activist, Emmy-nominated filmmaker and founder of The Webby Awards

Forage.

Gather.

100+ Recipes from
West Coast Forests,
Shores & Urban Spaces

Feast.

MARIA FINN

Photography by Marla Aufmuth

 SASQUATCH BOOKS | SEATTLE

CONTENTS

RECIPE LIST

THE FOREST

THE EDGE AND URBAN FORAGING

INTRODUCTION

*The world is a huge place. How will you know
where you fit in unless you explore beyond your
comfort zone?*

—SIR ERNEST SHACKLETON

~~~~~~~~~~~~~~~~~

Planet Earth's beauty and the pleasure found in wild foods are
everyone's birthright. Ripe berries and chanterelles for all! Going
out into nature to find your own food is a primal part of our being
and yet has grown unfamiliar. Sure, you may get stared at for snipping spruce tips or reaching into overgrown blackberry bushes as
if performing a deviant public act. But a deep part of us still yearns
for berry-stained hands and the sizzle of food cooking on live fire.
Foraging is a way to make space for beauty in our lives, and preparing delicious edibles creates pleasure.

Being outdoors is good for you in so many ways. It reduces
stress, heart rate, and risks of diabetes or cardiovascular disease,
and improves sleep. But there are the nonquantifiable reasons for
heading into nature that are just as important. It's fun and keeps us
learning, curious, and engaged with our surrounding world. And it
helps us tune in and connect to the ancient cycles of our planet.

This book guides you into the woods and to the water's edge for
an adventure with purpose. It helps you see delicacies hanging over
the sidewalk or slipping through the cracks. Harvesting wild food is
an unscripted experience that requires us to follow nature's rhythms
of tides and seasons, rain and dry spells. If we do this, she gives us

incredible, nutritious food for *free*. Those forty-five-dollar-a-pound porcini? You can go find your own! Pickle rose hips and oranges, make seaweed butter, ferment your own vinegar blends—you'll have a very esoteric pantry that makes the simplest dishes more intriguing. Find miner's lettuce and stinging nettles—delicious specialties that still have the bitter, sour, yummy complexity of food before it was dumbed down for uniformity in grocery stores.

Foraging is the antidote to our too-too-busy lives and crazy, convoluted, complex food systems. And when we are out in nature, we learn to live by nature's rules. Check the tides before heading out for clams or seaweed. Notice rain patterns for optimal mushroom hunting. Learn about the confluences of fresh and salt water, where native oysters love to live. What if we accepted the generosity of planet earth with reverence and passed it along? Could we then start becoming a keystone species that improves habitats for all other life on earth?

When going out into the wild to find your own food, you may get wet or muddy or scratched or scared. Often, you will get tired. You may find nothing, or so much you can barely carry it home. But it's in these dark hollows, amid bushwhacking or escaping waves in the impact zone, where you will meet parts of yourself you've long lost, and even discover new aspects of yourself.

Sharing the wild food you find with others is also sharing these newly discovered aspects of yourself with friends and family. The more time you spend in nature, the more you will recognize yourself, reflected back to you from a thousand different moments—rays of light filtering through branches, mushrooms opening to release their spores, ferns unfurling, the carcass of a deer left by a predator, the sting of a bee, a modest orchid, the hush of sunrise. No aspect is bad or good; they just are parts of a whole, and you'll start seeing them in yourself. Ecologist Rachel Carson wrote, "Each of us carries in our veins a salty stream in which the elements sodium, potassium and calcium are combined in almost the same proportions as seawater." In the book *Scent and the Scenting Dog,* William Syrotuck states that it's estimated our skin has the same bacterial content as the soil. We are fractals of planet earth and deep down, we crave nature.

This book encourages you to rewild yourself and eat inspired by our surrounding ecosystems. This I call "ecosystem-based eating." Create dishes according to the ecosystems where you find the food, and follow nature as a guide for what to eat. Does your plate look like an intertidal zone, a boreal forest?

HOW TO USE THIS BOOK

This book does not have any recipes where meat and poultry are the center of the plate. It's not intentionally a pescatarian or vegetarian cookbook. In the woods, there are nuts and fungi; at the coast, we find underwater seaweed, small fish, bivalves. I try to mimic nature as much as possible on the plate. I'm not a hunter. I'm not against ethical hunting for food. I just don't do it.

I strongly believe that food systems benefiting the earth are also good for our bodies—hello, oysters and truffles! And, by mimicking ecosystems, we have a deeper sense of the unique and beautiful places where we live. A big pork chop or chicken breast at the center of the plate doesn't tell a story of these landscapes we love. Wild plums, morel mushrooms, kombu, and fir tips tell the story I want to be a part of. This is why you'll find recipes organized by coastal, forest, and urban ecosystems. This book is plant-forward, low-meat, and regenerative-focused, with some gluten-free, keto-ish, and vegan options.

Think of this book as part instruction and part inspiration. It is by no means a comprehensive guide to wild foods, and it doesn't advocate trying to "live off the land" and eat primarily wild foods. There are too many people for that. Rather, the foraging tips,

recipes, and DIYs are meant to get you outside, interacting with the natural world and translating that experience in your food. If you just harvest salt once a year, every time you sprinkle it over your dishes, you'll have a memory of being at the ocean's edge, pelicans flying by in formation, the spout of a whale in the distance. The goal of this book is for you to fall in love with nature in the most visceral way possible—through food. The recipes are simple yet the ingredients a bit esoteric. Some you may be able to find seasonally at the farmers' market or grocery store, but the fun is in finding your own patches of rose hips and huckleberries.

MY COOKING CREDS

I have no formal training as a chef. I have not worked in a Michelin-starred restaurant or attended a culinary school. Food was not even a love language in my family. I grew up in a large Irish Catholic family in the Midwest during the "cream of mushroom soup" epoch. I thought of food as a vehicle for ketchup or melted Velveeta. I did have a lot of informal training as a cook. I worked the hot dog stand at All Star Wrestling and Monster Truck and Tractor pulls. I worked in restaurants for years. I bussed and then waited tables, and at times had shifts in the kitchen at the salad station or line; there, I tasted poached salmon and seared rack of lamb for the first time. Oysters were a wonderland. I learned to make hollandaise and what was meant by a chicken "breast" and that you couldn't cook them while they were still frozen. This was some cheffy stuff for a lit major in college.

After college, I headed to Alaska and crewed as a deckhand and cook on an all-female commercial salmon fishing boat—with pots and pans shifting in the waves, we were often down to cans of food that had long lost their labels and old pilot bread that was eerily still crisp despite decades on a ship and freshly caught wild salmon. I ate wild salmon every day for nine summers and it's still one of my favorite foods.

When I worked in field camps for the Alaska Department of Fish and Game, airplanes would drop boxes with SPAM and iceberg lettuce to us; the local Yupik natives taught me how to smoke salmon and cure the eggs, find wild spinach, and search the tundra for low-lying blueberry bushes and salmonberries.

When the salmon weren't running, I traveled, which did wonders to broaden my perspective on food. I also had the pleasure of working as a food writer for years, focusing on sustainability, particularly in seafood. Food is never just food. The where and the why matter. Give me the visionaries over the perfectionists. I'd much rather write about a commercial fisherwoman or permaculture farmer who is changing food systems to be more regenerative than the "ten best burgers" or celebrity chefs.

I began cooking professionally at Stochastic Labs in Berkeley, a residency and incubator for artists, scientists, and tech engineers. Feeding visionaries and hungry artists, I was allowed to be creative. The fractal artists showed me the math formulas they based their coding on, and I laser cut this into seaweed sheets and pita bread. When artists working to launch projects into space came to dinner, I researched what astronauts ate and made a menu inspired by this. When people who created CRISPR at UC Berkeley came, I threatened to feed them GMO salmon. Then COVID hit and I lost all my work.

So I adopted a truffle dog, Flora Jayne, and began training her to find these lusty, magical fungi. I wanted to take her to work with me, so I launched wild food camps, Flora & Fungi Adventures, where I teach people to forage and prepare food over an open fire. These are up and running all over the West Coast. It is a way to connect to wilderness, to seasons, to each other, and to ourselves.

I still have no formal training, but I make a large part of my living cooking. I also forage, preserve, and prepare wild foods in creative

ways. If I mess something up, say, chop vegetables unevenly because an unruly gang of raccoons is heading into camp, I call it a "rustic chop." If my pizzas are shaped like amoebas instead of round, I call them "flatbreads." I burn something a little, it's "blackened" or "charred."

I encourage you to go easy on yourself when cooking. Food is a persistent source of pleasure, and preparing it should be fun, not something you need to do perfectly. The mistakes are often how new dishes are born. As well, many herbs and other ingredients can be substituted for something you already have—so try that instead of going to the store and letting other produce wilt in the fridge. I think of this cookbook as a guide—there's lots of room for you to bring your own funky, creative self to it. Ultimately, cooking is an expression of love, and that is infinitely messy and imperfect.

WHAT MAKES A FORAGER?

Foraging Is a State of Mind

Money has no value here. Because there is no profit to be made from foraging, it tends to be controversial and often illegal for no real reason in many places. Knowing how to find or grow your own food is a form of radical independence and subversive living.

Foragers Are Up for Adventure

At its core, foraging is walking, ambling, observing. It's a slightly more exciting verb than "walking." But there's always the possibility of adventure: mud and tides coming in and waves crashing and getting lost in the woods or getting caught in a squall. And maybe a raccoon or two. Maybe a bear. Stay calm. You got this.

Foragers Follow Rules—and Question Rules

Many, many rules exist about what you can take from a piece of public land, when you can take it, how much, and what licenses you may need. Check with National Park Service and Fish and Wildlife websites to learn the rules before heading out. On private land, you always need permission. Foraging is strictly off-limits in some places, like marine protected areas where the intent is for the ecosystem to remain intact. At other times, rules can seem pretty random—it's illegal to pick a mushroom in all state parks in California except Salt Point. When I've asked officials why this is the case, there's some mumbling about how "walking off the paths to pick a mushroom will hurt the forest." This is a stretch. Somehow it's illegal for me to

BIODIVERSITY AND WILDFIRES

Currently, more than one million acres of Californian forests have been clear-cut, with an average of fifty thousand private acres of land being clear-cut each year. About 97 percent of California's ancient redwoods have been cut down for lumber. After clear-cutting, timber companies then apply heavy doses of herbicides and pesticides to the area, killing the soil and poisoning streams. They do this so that native vegetation cannot grow back and compete with the replanting of tree plantations with fir, pine, and redwood trees that are worth more as lumber. This practice of creating tree plantations means that most trees in our forests are the same age and the forest lacks biodiversity, which makes them much more susceptible to wildfires. Clear-cutting is a completely legal practice that contributes to the increasing number and intensity of wildfires, which threaten more than thirty-three million acres of land in California alone each year. It is a sociopathic assault on the natural world and the health of all creatures. Foraging mushrooms did not cause any of the problems we are currently facing.

pick a chanterelle while on an evening walk with my dog, which in no way harms the mycelium, let alone a tree. Yes, follow the rules, but take a look at the bigger picture and ask questions of those who make the rules.

Foragers Practice Self-Reliance

Have a compass you know how to read. Check the weather. Bring lots of water, snacks, some sunscreen, and a hat. Wear comfortable shoes and long socks. Tell someone where you are going and when you plan on returning. Bring insect repellent to keep ticks away. Wash up immediately upon leaving the woods to avoid poison oak rashes. If you're adventuring with a dog, a vet may be a few hours away. For my dog, I take hydrogen peroxide in case I need to make her throw up a mushroom that could be toxic. I also bring liquid charcoal to give her after she throws up to help clear toxins from her system. Pack Benadryl for yourself and your dog—if either of you ingests blue-green algae from river water or are bitten by a rattlesnake, this can save your lives long enough to get you to emergency care.

Foragers Respond to Abundance

It can be nothing, nothing, nothing, and then *bam*, morels all day long. Foragers preserve their often-short-lived bounty by drying; making salts, butters, pickles, jams, compotes, and ferments; or infusing booze.

Foragers Don't Waste

Use the whole dandelion and fish. Compost, turn your oyster shells into mulch, upcycle jars. Only buy something if you have exhausted other DIY options. If a recipe here calls for thyme and you have other kinds of herbs in the fridge, use those.

Foragers Don't Take More Than They Can Use

Know thyself. How many hours are you going to spend cleaning and hanging seaweed to dry? How many wild strawberries do you need? Will you eat all those porcini? With foraging, the work really starts when you get home with your bounty, so don't take more than you can process in the next few days.

Foragers Know That Food Tastes Better in the Wild

It's that simple. Cut open the sea urchin on the beach and pick out the *uni*, your feet still wet from the wave that made its way into your boots. Eat the ripe fig right off the tree and taste the warmth of the sun on it. You don't need a fancy cooking range or expensive chef's knife to enjoy wild food.

Foragers Embrace Uncertainty and Practice Gratitude

In nature we encounter uncertainty, which is one of our most pervasive fears, yet it opens our lives to unexpected wonders. Foraging is just one way to experience the beauty and generosity of the natural world. Entering it requires letting go of our expectations and replacing them with humility; even scientists don't know all the intricacies of how ecosystems work, let alone how they intersect with each other to create our biosphere. Nature invites us into uncertainty, and the more we appreciate the beauty of nature, the more we can embrace uncertainty in our lives.

THE

COAST

The cure for anything is salt water—
tears, sweat, or the sea.

—ISAK DINESEN

~~~~~~~~~~~~~

COASTAL GEAR LIST

- Tide chart, app, or good marine weather website
- Rubber boots or neoprene shoes
- One to two 5-gallon buckets
- Mesh bag
- Compost bags (for separating seaweed by species)
- Cheesecloth
- Scissors or garden clippers
- Cooler
- Layers of clothes
- Change of clothes (or at least socks in case they get wet)

We used to refer to the ocean and seafood as a chain and discussed our link in it. Now we are seeing that the connections are more like a web. From phytoplankton and seaweed to sharks and orcas, there are complex, interconnected feeding relationships that we are still learning about.

As well, a web shows that all life on earth is connected. We don't always know how. Here is where you enter the unknown—arrive at a tide pool at daybreak to find kombu; dig for clams at low tide; head to the rocky shores to drop a crab pot or toss a herring net. This section encourages you to enter the fascinating and delicious world of the intertidal zone. And so, as cooks and eaters, the unknown, the new, and the novel are our entry points. Foraging your own seafood can be as complex as contemplating the divine mechanisms of the universe, or as simple as pursuing our food the way a sea lion does—by responding to seasonal abundance and wily opportunism.

Seaweed

TANGLED CLUMPS OF SEAWEED STREWN ALONG beaches like fractal tales of offshore storms are indicators that the season is starting. When anchored in the water, they are pure poetry, swaying with the currents. These algae are vital to the well-being of the ocean. They are the basis of the marine food web; sea creatures need them for sustenance and protection.

Seaweed also reduces coastal erosion, buffers against waves, and filters excess nutrients from wastewater. It's a voracious sequester of carbon from the air and salt water. On land, it's nothing short of miraculous—researchers at UC Davis found that including seaweed in cow feed reduced their methane emissions by 82 percent.

No toxic seaweeds exist in the United States. They are all edible, though some taste better than others and some are thick and chewy in unappealing ways. Seaweed is a superfood. In fact, it's one of the most nutritious foods you can eat. Seaweed has vitamins, antioxidants, and omega-3s in spades. Scientists have found compounds in seaweed that help in weight loss and even fetal brain development when eaten by pregnant women.

The sex life of seaweed is rich and varied. It stands to reason that with such raucous sex lives, seaweed is a potent aphrodisiac. This is in part due to the high vitamin B content, which helps with hormone production, and iodine, which is libido-boosting, as well as manganese, a mineral known to help maintain a healthy sex drive.

So why don't we eat more seaweed? Outside of sushi restaurants, we rarely see it. And even many in the United States make sushi rolls with the nori wrappers inside the rice to please the anti-seaweed American palate. The discovery of umami—which means "delicious taste"—is thanks to kombu, a type of seaweed. This fifth flavor (the other four being salty, sweet, sour, and bitter) is rich, savory, and deeply satisfying. Mushrooms, cheese, anchovies—can all give depth to a dish that dances on our taste buds' pleasure centers. Yet seaweed still hasn't quite broken into our pantries the way other umami-rich foods have.

Infusing dairy with seaweed gives it a rich, minerally layer of flavor. Making fresh pasta with it adds an umami essence to simple dishes, and you can get creative by adding it to salads, including it in broths and soups, crumbling it over rice bowls for some crunch, and fermenting it with fruit. I've included only the most common culinary seaweeds in this section, but it's safe to taste other types when you're out there to see what you like.

Seaweed is even more amazing if you forage it yourself. With the sun rising, you can marvel at the tide pools and the sea creatures making the long, slow evolution to land. It's a sublime experience that gets translated into your dishes.

BEST PRACTICES FOR HARVESTING SEAWEED

1   Check local laws and regulations for foraging seaweed through the local Department of Fish and Wildlife, and make sure you aren't entering ecologically sensitive areas, like marine protected areas. In California you do not need a license; in Washington you do; and in certain parts of Alaska it is strictly forbidden to take even a piece of dead seaweed from the beach. The limits differ, but most are ten wet pounds—which is a lot more than you will want to clean and dry.

2   Stay away from areas that are heavily populated or have industrial or intensive agricultural runoff nearby.

3   Collect seaweed when the tide is low. Once it's dry on the beach, insects may be breaking it down, so gather it in the water, just below the tide line. Avoid any bits that look like something has been chewing on them.

4   Don't yank seaweed from the rock it's anchored to. Take scissors and snip, leaving at least three inches of the blade so it can grow back that season.

5   Leave the vast majority of the seaweed on the rock or in the kelp forest. Take a few blades from one cluster and then move to another one. Never pick a rock clean or cut down an entire bunch of seaweed. It is playing a critical role in the ecosystem.

6   Be careful when walking around rocks. Waves can splash through and knock you over or you can slip easily. You can step on fragile tide pool creatures and kill them. So step lightly and watch for waves!

7   Don't take more than you will use. It takes time to clean the seaweed and space to dry it, so be mindful of this when harvesting.

PROCESSING YOUR SEAWEED HARVEST

You can use your seaweed right away while it's fresh. You'll want to rinse it first in the ocean to remove critters, sand, and excess salt. Then you can give it a more thorough cleaning. To do this, either strain sea water through a cheesecloth to remove particles and then use for cleaning to keep the briny flavor, or you can rinse with tap water. This process is highly debated among seaweed foragers. Some think you wash off the umami and flavor with plain water, but it's a lot simpler and your seaweed will still be tasty.

To dry your seaweed, hang it from a clothing line outside or drape it on a pasta rack or screen in your house. (I use a baking screen on my foldable clothes-drying rack.) After it has dried all the way through, which usually takes a day or so, store in a lidded glass jar in a cool, dry place. It should last a year like this.

SEAWEED TYPES

Nori

Porphyra

This is the most well-known of seaweeds as it's used to wrap sushi rolls. However, these sheets are processed and pressed nori. Having fresh nori is a totally different experience. It's very light in texture with a mild, mineral flavor.

LOCATION: It grows on boulders in the high-water mark of the intertidal zone, so it's easier to access.

SEASON: Harvest late spring through summer at low tides.

BEST USES: Since nori is so thin, it has a nice mouthfeel and is great for making seaweed salads. It was commonly ground down into a type of "flour" for breads in Wales. Dried, it makes great chips. Just fry in hot oil and finish with a good salt or *gomasio*. Larger pieces, flash-fry and eat with fresh rice, brined salmon eggs, and slivers of avocado. It is also good as tempura.

Sea Lettuce

Ulva

Often referred to as "sea lettuce," *Ulva* do resemble the land plant with their uneven leaves and bright-green color. They're also very thin, and are often substituted for nori in a salad or flash-fried for chips.

LOCATION: Sea lettuce can be found in every ocean in the world, though it prefers cooler water. This type of algae grows in calm areas, so inner bays and estuaries are good places to look. Since they like still water, make sure it's a pristine area to forage from.

SEASON: Harvest in spring and early summer. They will still be young, tender, and less likely to have accumulated pollutants. Wash well as snails and other tide pool creatures like to live in the blades.

BEST USES: When dried, they have an almost truffle-like scent. These are my favorites for infusing cream and making butter or shredding and baking into bread. Use fresh within a few days, or dry and it's good for about a year. Great for seaweed salads, you can also flash-fry and make into chips or crumble over noodles and rice bowls.

Kelp/Kombu

Laminaria setchellii

Kombu is the Japanese term for the genus *Laminaria*, a category of brown algae or kelp. Some species of kelp are struggling due to climate change, but kombu is abundant along the West Coast and one of the most popular culinary seaweeds.

LOCATION: There are many types of kelp, and they tend to grow deeper in subtidal zones clustered in "forests." They're almost always anchored to a rock, so watch your footing and snip sparingly so they can grow back that season.

SEASON: Late spring through midsummer. As they age, their blades will start to fray and look chewed on.

BEST USES: The flavor of kombu is mildly salty with a green vegetable essence to it, on its own, but put into dishes and broths it transforms them into something far greater than the parts. Perfect for dashi and other soup stocks, kombu is also highly versatile. I mix it with salt, put it in gomasio or blend into butter to add umami, and sometimes use it as a secret ingredient when fermenting. It's been said that when it's cooked with beans, it takes out the gas inducing properties of beans. When dry, kombu often has a white powdery substance on it—these are flavorful, umami-rich compounds, so don't wipe them off!

Wakame

Undaria pinnatifida, Alaria marginata

Wakame has a stronger mineral flavor than kombu and thicker fronds than nori; it's a popular culinary seaweed. The species of wakame known as *Undaria pinnatifida* is invasive in California; it most likely hitched a ride over from its native waters near Asia on the hull of ships. It's golden brown and has a thick stipe down the center. It can grow up to eight feet long in dense forests that crowd out native species. Our native wakame is *Alaria marginata*. These are brown and smaller, from two to six feet. They are also called winged kelp. Both species have a midrib that runs along their length, with wavy edges called wings.

LOCATION: Wakame is found in the mid-intertidal zone. If you are 100 percent sure that it's the invasive species and not good for local habitat, you don't have to adhere to the ½ rule. If it's native, snip sparingly.

SEASON: Harvest late spring through summer.

BEST USES: This is the seaweed most commonly found in miso soup and seaweed salads. You'll want to cut out the stipe, since it's thick and has a tough texture. You can chop and stir-fry wakame with ginger or use to flavor soups.

Bladder Wrack

Fucus distichus

These brown algae are found growing from boulders in the high intertidal zone, near nori. Their blades are thick and crunchy. It's very high in iodine, so great if you have thyroid issues. But it may be contraindicated with other medications, so check before you consume it. It can also have a strong iodine aftertaste, so it's good to get it while it's still fairly young and has a clean flavor.

LOCATION: Bladder wrack is easy pickings. They are on boulders and among mussel beds.

SEASON: Harvest late spring and early summer.

BEST USES: Try fresh, young bladder wrack in salads and teas. A little later in the season, try it pickled with fresh ginger and added to a salad or over rice. Traditionally, it is made into a medicinal tea.

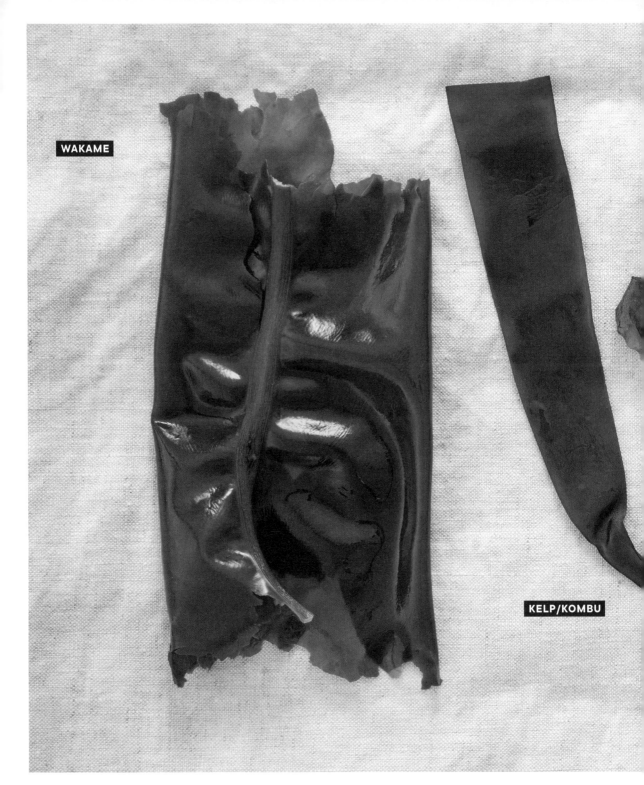

WAKAME

KELP/KOMBU

SEA LETTUCE

BLADDER WRACK

NORI

Seaweed, Seed, Oat, and Nut Bread

MAKES 1 LOAF

1½ cups rolled oats

½ cup dried seaweed (such as nori, kombu, sea lettuce, wakame, or any variation), torn into small pieces

½ cup raw pumpkin seeds

½ cup raw sunflower seeds

½ cup raw hazelnuts

⅓ cup sesame seeds

¼ cup raw almonds

¼ cup ground flaxseed meal

5 tablespoons whole psyllium husks

2 tablespoons chia seeds

1½ cups water

3 tablespoons coconut oil (or ghee/butter)

There's a pre-famine saying in Ireland: "Potatoes, children, seaweed. That was the order of care for the women of the house." You'll find brown soda bread with seaweed in Ireland or laverbread (oatmeal and nori cakes) in Wales. So when I first started making a popular version of the seed-and-nut bread, I realized that the oats would allow the mineral flavors of seaweed to shine. By adding seaweed, the bread has a savory layer. Also, unlike most baking, you can substitute your preferred nuts and seeds here. The only ingredients that are nonnegotiable are the psyllium husks and oats, as they bind it all together. I've also found that cooling and storing this for a day in the fridge helps make it less crumbly. Try it with the Seaweed Butter (page 28) and Preserved Anchovies (page 80) or cashew butter and Raspberry and Chamomile Jam (page 229).

In a large mixing bowl, combine all the dry ingredients and mix.

In a small saucepan over medium heat, combine the water and coconut oil until the oil has melted.

Pour the oil mixture into the dry ingredients and combine until everything is completely soaked and the dough becomes very thick.

Line a bread loaf pan with parchment paper and fill with the dough, pressing into the sides and smoothing out the top.

Let sit out on the counter for at least 2 hours, or all day or overnight.

Preheat the oven to 350 degrees F. ⟶

Place the loaf pan in the oven on the middle rack and bake for 30 minutes.

Remove the bread from the loaf pan, place it upside down directly on the rack, and bake for another 30 to 40 minutes. The bread is done if it sounds hollow when tapped. Let cool completely before slicing.

Store the bread in a tightly sealed container for up to 5 days. It freezes well too—slice before freezing for quick-and-easy toast! (Note: This bread slices better with a non-serrated knife.)

SEAWEED GODDESS

The pagan Celtic goddess Brigid, now a patron Catholic saint of Ireland, is associated with seaweed. According to lore, oystercatchers covered her with it to hide her from pursuers. She's also a goddess of poetry and beer brewing and seems just overall fun to hang with. On February 1, it's tradition in rural, coastal areas of Ireland to harvest seaweed in celebration of Saint Brigid and the first day of spring. This was most often used to fertilize soil, but seaweed has made its way into many foods of the British Isles.

Campfire Dashi-Poached Eggs with Vegetable Hash

MAKES 4 SERVINGS

- 4 cups Morel Mushroom and Kombu Dashi (recipe follows) or store-bought
- ½ pound purple sweet potatoes, cut into thin rounds
- 10 fresh shiitake mushrooms, sliced
- 8 medium eggs
- 2 cups stemmed and roughly chopped dark leafy greens (like kale or Swiss chard)
- 4 scallions, sliced lengthwise and chopped into small pieces
- 2 to 4 inches of fresh or reconstituted kombu, cut into strips
- ¼ cup tamari
- 2 tablespoons mirin
- Kosher salt
- Freshly ground black pepper
- Seaweed Gomasio, for garnish (page 83)

The first time I poached eggs over a campfire at seaweed camp, a lot of people thought I couldn't do it. They shared their doubts politely, like, "Really? Are you sure you want to *poach* the eggs?" I'm like, "Hold my coffee!" The key to poaching eggs anywhere is to first crack them into a small bowl; I do it two at a time, but if you're feeling ambitious you could try more. This way, you can make a little whirlpool in the dashi broth and then slip the eggs into the center of it with no yolk breakage.

Make a fire and let the wood burn down to a low flame, just before coals. Set a large cast-iron skillet over the fire.

Heat up the dashi broth until you see a few bubbles rising.

Add the sweet potatoes and cook for about 10 minutes, or until soft, and then add the mushrooms.

Crack 2 eggs into a small bowl.

Make space in the vegetables. If you can, make a little whirlpool in the broth for the eggs. Carefully slip the eggs into the broth. Repeat until the rest of the eggs are nestled in their whirlpools.

Cook over a gentle simmer. When the eggs are almost done—meaning a soft yolk but firm white—add the greens, scallions, and kombu and gently stir. Don't break the eggs!

Add the tamari and mirin.

When the whites of the eggs start to solidify, scoop the vegetables into each bowl and top with 2 eggs and a ladleful of broth.

Season with salt and pepper to taste. Finish with a sprinkle of gomasio.

MOREL MUSHROOM AND KOMBU DASHI

MAKES 1 QUART

3 cups water

1 piece of kombu, about 2 inches wide and 4 to 6 inches long

¾ cup dried morels

Note: I like to puree the morels and kombu with a bit of sesame oil, garlic, and tamari and blend it back into the broth for a deeply delicious soup.

Dashi is a simple, subtle, and fragrant broth with a foundation of kombu seaweed. Traditionally in Japan it's made with kombu and bonito, a fish in the tuna family that is smoked and then shaved into superthin pieces. Often shiitake mushrooms or even anchovies are added to layer in the rich umami experience of this broth. I like to use my dried morel mushrooms for this, because morels make everything dank and delicious due to their deep flavor, which out-umamis even the shiitake and anchovies. So this umami superstorm can be enjoyed on its own and is also a great basis for soup. You can use it for poaching fish or vegetables to layer the flavor.

In the water, steep the kombu overnight at room temperature.

In a medium pot on the stove top over medium-low heat, add the water-kombu combo.

When the water is hot, with bubbles rising from the bottom, but not at a rolling boil, add the morels.

Simmer for 10 minutes, then turn off the heat and let steep for 5 to 10 minutes.

Strain out the morels and kombu.

Seaweed Pasta with Confit Tomatoes and Smoked Anchovy Butter

*MAKES 4 MAIN
COURSES OR 8 SIDE
DISHES*

FOR THE PASTA:

2 tablespoons dried
wakame seaweed (or
kombu, sea lettuce,
or a combination of all
three), finely ground

2 tablespoons
extra-virgin olive oil

2 cups unbleached
all-purpose flour (00
flour if possible)

2 cups semolina flour

4 large eggs

FOR THE CONFIT:

2 pints cherry tomatoes

5 cloves garlic, peeled

⅓ cup extra-virgin
olive oil

3 sprigs fresh thyme

1 sprig fresh rosemary

1 teaspoon kosher salt

1 teaspoon freshly
ground black pepper

1 teaspoon red chili
flakes

½ cup Smoked Anchovy
Butter (page 78)

Fresh pasta is an entirely different experience than store-bought. It's silkier and thicker, and adding seaweed to it creates umami depth and beauty to your dish. It's also really fun to make pasta with a group of people, which can be a bonding experience; the more hands for holding and hanging and rolling out the pasta, the better it seems to be.

Confit is a French method of slow cooking food in fat at lower temperatures. Although this dish already has savory and deep flavors, you could punch it up with spot prawns sautéed in garlic, butter, and white wine. Pancetta would be good as well. If you don't have the Smoked Anchovy Butter on hand, just use regular butter.

TO MAKE THE PASTA DOUGH:

First, put the seaweed flakes in the olive oil so they soften.

Pour the flours in a large bowl and make a well in the center. Crack the eggs into the center of the well and mix them by hand or use a stand mixer.

Slowly add the seaweed mixture as you blend the flour for 8 to 10 minutes.

Flatten the dough into disks, wrap them in plastic, and let rest for half an hour in the fridge.

Remove the dough from the fridge and divide it into four equal parts. Keep the sections you aren't using covered with a cloth so they don't dry out. $\longrightarrow$

Scatter flour onto your work surface; then flatten out one of the quarters of dough into an oval shape. Flour both sides.

Put the dough through the pasta machine on the thickest setting. When it's flatter, almost sheetlike, fold it into thirds, and repeat two more times.

Put the rolled dough through the pasta machine on a noodle setting; there's usually a thin spaghetti and a thicker fettuccine. Roll it through, and then gently lay the pasta onto a tray sprinkled with semolina flour. If the pasta feels sticky, you can hang it on a pasta rack or open a cupboard and hang it over the door.

Let it dry until you're ready to boil it.

TO MAKE THE CONFIT:

Preheat the oven to 300 degrees F.

In a large baking dish, toss the tomatoes and garlic with the olive oil, fresh herbs (whole), salt, pepper, and chili flakes.

Bake for 1 hour and 45 minutes, or until the tomatoes burst and the garlic is translucent.

When cool enough to handle, roughly chop the garlic and tomatoes and then return to the confit sauce.

To cook the pasta, bring a large pot of salted water to a boil. Add the pasta and cook for 4 to 5 minutes, or until al dente.

Drain the pasta, rinse, and return to the pot. Toss with the anchovy butter and confit.

Seaweed and Citrus Salad with Mulberry-Kombu Vinaigrette

MAKES 4 SERVINGS

FOR THE VINAIGRETTE:

3 tablespoons extra-virgin olive oil

2 tablespoons fresh Meyer lemon juice (from about 1 small to medium lemon)

1 tablespoon Mulberry-Kombu Vinegar (recipe follows) or apple cider vinegar

1 teaspoon tahini

1 teaspoon grated fresh ginger, skins removed

1 teaspoon maple syrup

¼ teaspoon freshly ground black pepper

½ teaspoon kosher salt

Seaweed salad often means strips of wakame in a sugary dressing. Most often what people are tasting is the sugar, not the seaweed. A salad made entirely of seaweed will not have the flavors and mouth-feel we've come to expect in a salad, and you definitely don't want a big dinner salad of only seaweed—and in restaurants, a high-quality one would be too costly to serve.

Rather, build a salad with many dimensions and add seaweed to it for some oceany notes. And beauty matters, particularly when it comes to food. I'm convinced that people will think a beautiful dish is far more delicious than a meh-looking one. With different textures, shapes, and colors, plus the surprise of citrus with seaweed, this salad becomes a multifaceted, multi-crunch experience.

And a note on my salad proportions—I like to eat salad until my jaw hurts. So they're pretty big.

In a small bowl, whisk all the vinaigrette ingredients together. Tahini can really thicken a dressing, so if it's too thick to pour easily, add water and continue whisking until it runs thinner. ⟶

FOR THE SALAD:

4 cups mild-flavored salad greens, like red leaf lettuce, Little Gem, or miner's lettuce

2 loosely packed cups frilly mustard greens, preferably a mix of red and green

1 cup chopped purple savoy cabbage

1 cup fresh peas, blanched

1 medium raw yellow beet, peeled, halved, and shaved on a mandoline into very thin half-moons

½ cup wet nori, chopped into bite-size pieces

½ cup wet sea lettuce, chopped into bite-size pieces

½ cup kumquats, thinly sliced and seeded

⅓ cup Pickled Bladder Wrack (page 27)

⅓ cup blue borage blossoms, for garnish (optional)

1 tablespoon Seaweed Gomasio (page 83) or toasted black sesame seeds, for garnish

1 teaspoon finishing salt

In a large salad bowl, add the salad greens, mustard greens, cabbage, peas, beet, nori, sea lettuce, kumquats, and bladder wrack and drizzle with the vinaigrette. Toss with tongs to combine all the ingredients, and make sure the dressing is evenly coating everything.

Serve the salad on four plates and sprinkle with the borage blossoms, gomasio, and finishing salt.

2 cups mulberries,
  rinsed

1 medium piece of
  kombu

4 cups water

½ cup sugar or honey
  (or a combination of
  the two)

½ cup organic, raw
  apple cider vinegar
  with some of the vin-
  egar mother left in

MULBERRY-KOMBU VINEGAR

This recipe was brainstormed around a fire at a seaweed camp.
We were geeking out about ways to ferment seaweed. Someone
suggested this combination. I love mulberries—they were the first
food I ever foraged, as there was a tree in my childhood backyard.
This vinegar combines mulberries' sticky purple sweetness with the
salty umami of kombu. The effect is a fruity yet not sweet, complex
layered vinegar that's perfect for dressings and shrubs.

———————————————————

Sterilize a 32-ounce glass container by filling it with very hot water or
putting it through the dishwasher.

Put the mulberries, kombu, water, and sugar in the jar; you don't need
to stem or sort the mulberries. Some people suggest not rinsing them
so they ferment better, but I do give them a quick rinse to get the bugs
out. Literally.

Cover the glass jar with a piece of cheesecloth held in place with a
rubber band, or a two-piece fermentation lid loosely screwed on.

Anywhere from 2 to 5 days, you should see bubbles forming. This
means the fermentation is working.

Strain the mulberries and kombu from the jar. Put the liquid back into
the jar and add the vinegar.

Place the jar in a cool, dry place for 2 to 6 months. The vinegar will
develop more depth of flavor as time goes on, and it will be good
for years.

Pickled Bladder Wrack

MAKES ONE
16-OUNCE JAR

1 cup fresh bladder wrack, or ½ cup dried bladder wrack

½ cup apple cider vinegar

½ cup water

1 tablespoon sugar

1 tablespoon kosher salt

These are great to have on hand to add to salad or put on the Sockeye Salmon Gravlax (page 165) or a herring board. The texture of bladder wrack makes for a crunchy pickle.

———————————————

Put the bladder wrack in a clean glass jar.

In a small nonreactive saucepan (use ceramic, enamel, glass, plastic, or stainless steel) over medium heat, combine the vinegar, water, sugar, and salt and cook just until the sugar and salt dissolve.

Remove the brine from the heat and let cool to room temperature.

Pour the brine into the jar over the bladder wrack.

Cover and store in the fridge for 30 days or process the jar in a water-bath canner, where it will keep for up to a year.

DIY: Rum and Seaweed Bitters

———————————————

Okay, salty people, this is for you. Fill a mason jar with seaweed—go ahead and mix it up: kombu, bladder wrack, nori, and wakame all work—and top it off with rum. Cover and store in a cabinet for a month. Strain and put your bitters in a jar.

Seaweed Butter from Scratch

**MAKES ONE ROUGHLY
5-INCH LOG**

⅓ cup (tightly packed)
dried sea lettuce
(*Ulva*)

1 pint grass-fed, organic
heavy cream

2 to 4 cups ice water

Flaky sea salt or Sea-
weed Gomasio (page
83), for finishing

You can infuse cream with seaweed and make your own butter out of it. The most amazing seaweed butter I've tasted was made by the chef Matthew Kammerer of Harbor House Inn in Mendocino. He explained this sorcery by way of holding a jar of dried sea lettuce to my nose; it had a sublime, rich, truffle-like scent. This is what he uses to infuse his butter, and now I do too. Note, he's a Michelin-starred chef who makes cultured butter and his process is way more involved than mine, so I adapted it into a Butter 101 version. You can add dulse and wakame and substitute other seaweeds, but sea lettuce is my favorite for infusing cream for homemade butter. Seaweed butter adds fairy dust to all bread.

Soak the sea lettuce in the cream overnight in the fridge.

Strain the cream through a tightly woven colander, pressing it all through with the back of a spoon. Allow small seaweed pieces to flow into the cream for aesthetics and added flavor. Compost the soaked seaweed.

Pour the cream into a blender or food processor and blend for 3 to 6 minutes. It will turn from whipped cream to a separated, beaded consistency—anyone who has ruined whipped cream by beating it too long will recognize this. Keep whipping it. Eventually the liquid will separate. Stop the blender, scrape the sides, then blend more.

Strain off the buttermilk. (If desired, you can save that for other things, like a seaweed buttermilk dressing or to use in biscuits.)

Put the solid butter into a clean glass bowl with space for the ice water.

Now rinse the butter. This takes out the casein, a protein in milk, that can cause your butter to go rancid. (Commercially produced butter is washed with either a chlorinated rinse or lactic acid for preservation.) Washing also makes the texture more velvety. To rinse, pour ½ cup of the ice water into the butter. Move the butter around, or "agitate" it, and then pour off the liquid. Do this a few more times, until the ice water runs clear.

Put your butter into a sieve and let all the liquid drain. Then work out the remaining liquid. You can do this several ways—put it into a cheese-cloth and squeeze or use a large spoon to rub over the surface, pressing it out. Or squeeze with your bare hands.

Once it has a thick consistency with no visible liquid beading, store in a covered ramekin in the fridge or use right away. Or, using plastic wrap, roll it into a log and store in the fridge. To freeze, store in a small mason jar, leaving ¼ inch of space at the top.

When ready to use, slice the butter off into rounds like you'd find at a fancy restaurant and garnish with a few flakes of sea salt or gomasio.

VARIATION: COMPOUND SEAWEED BUTTER

MAKES 1 TO 2 LOGS

1 cup (2 sticks) salted butter, softened

1 scant tablespoon dried seaweed (such as a combination of sea lettuce, nori, wakame, and a little kombu), ground into small flakes

Use dried seaweed for this. One thing I like to do is give the seaweed a little time over a fire, or a smoker, or just toast it lightly in a pan on the stove. Then grind it into small flakes with a spice grinder.

In a large bowl, add the butter and seaweed and mix thoroughly with a fork or your clean hands.

Once combined, store the seaweed butter in a covered ramekin in the fridge and let it firm up. Or using plastic wrap, roll it into a log and refrigerate or freeze.

Creatures of the Intertidal Zone

COOKING YOUR CRAB OR MUSSELS OR spot prawns or oysters on a beach, with the sound of waves splashing the rocky shoreline, is deep pleasure. Anything you catch will taste that much better. And you'll bring yourself into the food web in an intimate way. I haven't included many of the lesser-known barnacles or other edible, but more obscure creatures, because there are scant studies that show the impact of harvesting. I've also not included larger finfish like rockfish or lingcod that you could feasibly catch with a fishing pole from the rocks. I am including just the smaller ones that you would throw a net or a Sabiki rig for, like anchovies. The goal is for you to become familiar with your waterways and coastline and feel a sense of connection and stewardship to them. As well, this section aims for meals that look like a tide pool and taste like a squall traveling over the sea.

BIVALVES

The history of our coasts could be told with oysters, mussels, and clams. Massive middens, or oyster, mussel, and clam shell mounds, along the Salish Sea and the San Francisco Bay are evidence of Indigenous people's fondness for shellfish of the intertidal zone. In the 1800s, America's oyster carts were as ubiquitous as today's hot dog stands. Oysters were once America's most common and beloved source of protein. People who lived along bays foraged during low tide for seaweed, bivalves, and shellfish to keep their families fed.

Along with feeding the masses, bivalves keep ecosystems thriving. They are filter feeders, consuming naturally occurring algae, allowing plankton and eelgrass more sunlight, creating vital habitat for sea creatures, and improving water quality.

Harvest bivalves infrequently and responsibly. Don't take too much and be super mindful of not harming their ecosystem. Rather than a subsistence food source, think of it as an educational adventure that connects you to the ecosystem and the way people used to live with the rhythm of the land and sea. And if you don't find any, you can purchase bivalves from your local fishmonger. They are a great, regenerative seafood choice.

Oysters

Besides being a key part of the Pacific Northwest ecosystem, oysters also contour the bottoms of bays and offer protection from swell surge and sea level rise.

Unfortunately, during the gold rush in California, the demand for oysters by miners, along with silt and toxins from the mining, destroyed the oysters in the San Francisco Bay. So Olympia oysters were shipped from Seattle. This, along with pollution, put pressure on this native population, and vast oyster beds in Willapa Bay and other areas in the Pacific Northwest were overharvested. So non-native oysters were imported from the East Coast and then from Japan. These grew much larger, much faster. The Olympia oyster was all but forgotten in the food world. But as coastal cities face sea level rise, there is a renewed interest in our native wild oyster. Atlantic and Pacific oysters can't breed on their own along the West Coast of the United States, so they won't form the oyster reefs we once had. As well, an increasingly acidic ocean from climate change means that the spat, or tiny oyster larvae, of the imports have a difficult time developing shells. In a study at Oregon State, they found our native oysters are more resilient in this time of climate change.

Communities along Puget Sound and the San Francisco Bay are turning to oyster reefs and living coastlines to help mitigate storm surge and rising waters. Indigenous people along the Pacific coast have been returning to the ancient tradition of building clam gardens so the bivalves can flourish. And we've all become more aware of not polluting the waters we rely on. The bivalve's time has come again. Aqua farms producing oysters, clams, seaweed, and mussels are a new approach to growing regenerative food. So why take and eat them from the wild? I would suggest doing so infrequently and sparingly. Consider it an adventure and a gesture that connects you to the intertidal zone while also teaching you about it.

In Oregon, it's illegal to harvest wild oysters, yet the great state of Washington seeds oyster beaches for recreational oyster picking. (It's called picking, not foraging, in Washington.) Hood Canal is a hot spot for picking as well as other pristine places where fresh water meets the sea. Make sure you take only oysters that are over 2½ inches long and leave your oyster shells behind—so eat them raw on the spot, or build a fire on the beach. Limits for how many you can eat are posted at the sites.

Most people have heard the adage to only eat oysters in the months that have an *r* in them—September through March. This started when there wasn't refrigeration, but now, as long as they're kept cold, it's safe to eat oysters in the summer. However, the waters are warmer and often oysters are spawning, so they can be milky and not as crisp and mineral-tasting. My favorite months for picking them are February and March—they are rich with nutrients, crisp from the cold waters, and seem to have a pre-spawn je ne sais quoi.

Clams

Digging for clams requires the lowest tides possible, so look for a -1.5 to -2 or below. Make your way out into the intertidal zone, feet clad in rubber boots, shovel and pail in hand, until you see a wee waterspout, preferably a cacophony of them. For the smaller clams, like littlenecks, Manila, and butter, you dig just behind the hole the water shoots from and scoop up to uncover a cluster of them, if lucky. The largest of all clams, the phallic geoduck, can be found along the West Coast and fetches big dollars on the seafood market. It makes a delicious sashimi, but these bivalves live up to a hundred years old, so I don't really have the heart to kill them.

One of the most exciting clams in the Pacific Northwest is the razor. Catching razor clams is an extreme sport in the world of clamming. Many people choose to use a clam "gun," which is a PVC plastic pipe with a handle. This seems less rigorous than digging right next to the spout of water so you don't break their shells, dropping to your knees, and reaching into the cold, wet sand to grab them as they dive away from you. But I did the latter while living in Alaska—and often found myself belly down on the wet, cold sand, holding on to a razor clam with everything I had, which was diving down for dear life. The razor clams often prevailed. But when you get ahold of one and gently wriggle them up through the sand without breaking the shell or cutting your hand, you feel so victorious. They are delicious but large, about six inches across, so you'll want to clean them first, as they've got a bellyful of brown gunk and internal organs. They often go into chowder or are sautéed/deep-fried as strips. All the clams you can forage on the West Coast are fun to find and delicious, but they do require cleaning.

Mussels

Mussels are the lowest-hanging fruit in the world of bivalve foraging. Mussels filter plankton from the water to grow their shells, and the nutrients they excrete feed the local algae. Mussels web over rocky outcrops in splotchy patterns by using threads called byssus and secreting a sort of superglue; these bivalves dominate the upper part of intertidal zones as starfish will eat them in the lower parts. Their threads and glue, not to mention crashing waves, can make it difficult to remove them from the rocks, but they are plentiful along the coast, and delicious. In California, there's a quarantine on mussels from May through October. This is because the ocean water warms up (relatively speaking) during these months and the threat of a toxic algal bloom is higher during this time. Everyone should check with their local Fish and Wildlife on regulations and to make sure that mussels are safe to eat before foraging them.

BEFORE COOKING
WITH BIVALVES

INSPECT: Make sure clams, mussels, and oysters do not have broken shells. Their shells should be closed. They should smell fresh, like the sea. This means they are alive; dead bivalves should be tossed. If purchasing them, they should come with their tags that tell where and when they were harvested.

STORE: Since these guys are alive, they need to breathe, so you don't want to store them in an airtight bag. Even if you buy them and the fishmonger wraps them in plastic, remove it when you get home. The best way to store them is to line a pan with a damp paper towel. Layer the bivalves in the dish, and then cover them with another damp paper towel. For oysters, keep the cup side down so their "liquor" is preserved. Keep them in the fridge until you're ready to use them. If you are camping, they should be in a cooler; however, do not let them sit in melted ice water. Never let bivalves sit in fresh water in a cooler or the fridge for any length of time. They will die and then make you sick when you eat them.

PURGE: If you wild harvest clams (or even purchase them), they may have quite a bit of grit both inside and on their shells. Put them in a bowl of cold water and sea salt—two tablespoons of salt for every quart of water—for thirty minutes. They will spit out their grit. Once out of the salted water, rub any grit off their shells and give them a quick rinse. Mussels and oysters may not need to purge, but they will need to be rinsed. If there's any beard left on the mussels, cut or yank that off by pulling down on it with a firm, fast tug, and then rinse them well. Give oysters a quick rinse in the shell before opening.

Fire-Roasted Butter Clams with Seaweed Gremolata

MAKES 4 SERVINGS

5 pounds clams, or about 1 pound per person

2 cups Seaweed Gremolata (recipe follows)

These clams are good alone but can be served over linguini or buckwheat soba noodles, alongside toasted artisan bread. Any clams work for this, but I prefer them medium to smallish, like butter clams. I love this recipe as a one-pot dish when car camping. Make the gremolata in advance and store in a lidded container. It can also be frozen.

Heat a frying pan over a wood fire cooked down to coals. (You can also use a grill at home.) Test by flicking water on it to see if it sizzles.

Add clams in a single layer. (You may have to make them in two batches.) They will start to open as they cook and release salt water, which will sizzle in the pan and burn off.

When they are all open, if you like them chewier, wait about 30 more seconds and then remove from the fire. If you like them soft and more tender, take them off as soon as they open.

Put them in serving bowls, top with the gremolata, and toss.

If serving with linguini or soba noodles, cook the noodles according to package directions and toss with a few tablespoons of gremolata. Then put the clams over the noodles. Serve and enjoy!

1 cup extra-virgin olive oil

1 cup fresh tender herbs (such as a combination of parsley, basil, sage, and oregano), stemmed and roughly chopped

½ cup fresh seaweed (such as kombu, nori, and wakame, or any combination), roughly chopped, or ¼ cup dried flakes

Zest of 1 medium lemon

Juice of 1 medium lemon

2 large cloves garlic, minced

½ teaspoon red chili flakes

½ teaspoon kosher salt

¼ teaspoon freshly ground pepper

SEAWEED GREMOLATA

This is a simple green herb sauce that's tangy from lemon, a little spicy and garlicky, but made with seaweed so it has a little more mineral flavor and depth. Fresh herbs you have on hand in any combination work well; chives or thyme can also be used. I find that rosemary can be overpowering, but a little is good, and garnishing with the blue rosemary blossoms adds a lovely and light touch.

Drizzle the gremolata over drier fish that needs a little fat, like lingcod or halibut, or work it into aioli for a quick, easy accompaniment to artichokes. I also like to drizzle it over half an avocado with some *ikura* for a quick breakfast or lunch.

Put all the ingredients into a blender and pulse a few times. Or you can mix by hand for a chunkier gremolata.

Making this a day in advance will allow the flavors to blend and the garlic to mellow a bit.

Store in a lidded container for up to 2 weeks.

Steamed Clams with Pea Shoots and Green Garlic

MAKES 4 SERVINGS

¼ cup unsalted butter

2 tablespoons minced green garlic (see note)

5 pounds of Manila or littleneck clams, cleaned and purged

2 cups white wine

4 stems fresh thyme

½ cup high-heat oil (like avocado or peanut)

2 pounds pea shoots

1 tablespoon tamari

1 lemon, cut into wedges, and juice from half

Kosher salt

Freshly ground black pepper

½ cup wild mustard or wild onion flowers, for garnish

Note: Green garlic is much milder than older garlic, so reduce the amount of traditional garlic you are using if you can't find any green garlic.

In the spring you'll find pea shoots and mustard flowers near wineries and farms as many places use them as a cover crop to replenish their soil, and the farms rarely have any interest in the peas and mustard plants themselves. These plants go feral easily and often hop to nearby roadsides, so don't trespass on the farms, but look nearby. I like to cook the pea shoots at high heat, apart from the clams, as their crisp texture is a big part of their allure and steaming them would diminish this. The mustard flowers just make it pretty.

While five pounds of clams sounds like a lot for four people, they are mostly shells, and when buying these, they often come in five-pound bags. If you're foraging, just come as close as you can.

In a large saucepan over medium heat, add the butter and garlic.

When the butter is melted, add the clams, white wine, and thyme and cover with a lid.

In a deep skillet over medium to high heat, add the oil.

Quickly stir-fry the pea shoots on high heat, for just a minute or two. They should be bright green and crisp. Remove and put into a bowl.

Toss with the tamari, lemon juice from half a lemon, salt, and pepper. (Keep the tamari really light, it should just be a light accent to the greens, not overwhelm them.)

Scoop out the clams, including some of the wine-butter sauce as well, and place these over the pea shoots.

Garnish with the mustard or wild onion flowers and lemon wedges.

Razor Clam Chowder with Saffron, Fennel, and Leeks

1 large Yukon gold
potato, diced into
¼-inch cubes

4 strips of bacon

1 medium yellow onion,
· diced

1 small fennel bulb, diced

1 cup leeks, cleaned
and chopped into
half-moons

1 cup clam juice—from
cleaning the clams

8 to 10 saffron threads

1 bay leaf

Kosher salt

Freshly ground black
pepper

1 cup whole milk

1 cup heavy cream, or
2 cups half-and-half
or nondairy milk

8 to 10 razor clams, or
about 1 cup chopped
clams (if using steam-
ers in the shell, 2 to
3 pounds)

2 fennel fronds, for
garnish

Espelette pepper or
smoked paprika, for
garnish

There are many ways to clean a razor clam. Just search YouTube and you will be regaled for many seven-minute segments on razor clam cleaning. You can either slice them out of their shells or put them in boiling hot water for about ten seconds and then run them under cold water and their shells will come off. If you boil them, save some of the water, and if you clean them raw, do your best to collect the juices for use in the chowder. After they're clean, roughly chop them.

If you don't have razor clams, use steamers or even canned clams. For steamers, I like to leave them in the shell and add at the very end. They only take a few minutes to steam open and their salty juices blend into the chowder. It's much easier than removing them from the shells and makes for a fun way to pick through the chowder. The saffron in this recipe has a subtle floral flavor, the bacon is stealth umami, and the clams are delicious ocean—flavor-wise, it's a biosphere in a bowl. Enjoy while watching autumn storms blow in from the sea.

Bring a large pot of salted water to a boil and cook the potatoes until tender but still firm. Drain and set aside.

In a large heavy-bottomed pan over high heat, cook the bacon and then remove from the pan with a slotted spoon. Chop into small pieces and set aside.

Add the onion, fennel, and leeks to the bacon fat and cook over medium-high heat until softened. If there's not enough bacon fat, add butter or olive oil, as needed.

Add the potatoes, clam juice, saffron, bay leaf, salt, and pepper to the onion mixture. Cook over medium heat until the potatoes start to soften and thicken the chowder, about 15 minutes.

Reduce the heat and add the milk, cream, bacon, and clams. If you are using steamers in their shells, cover the pot. Let it simmer on low heat for about 15 minutes. Check to make sure the bottom doesn't burn. It should thicken and the clam shells should open.

Divide into bowls and garnish with the fennel fronds and Espelette pepper.

Flaming Pine Needle Mussels

MAKES 4 SERVINGS

5 pounds of mussels, scrubbed clean

½ cup butter, cut into ¼-inch cubes

2 garlic cloves, minced

2 cups white wine

1 large bag of very dry pine needles gathered somewhere dogs are unlikely to have peed (see note)

1 dried rosemary branch, fennel, or other wild herbs (optional)

2 crusty baguettes, for serving

This is my favorite way to prepare mussels. It's dramatic and delicious and perfect over a fire at the beach. The classic way in coastal France to prepare *terrée de moules* is to set the mussels in a circular mandala, standing upright, their opening facing upward, and covered with a pile of pine needles. Light the pine needles on fire, and as the needles flame and burn down to ash, they cook the mussels and flavor them with a smoky pine essence. I place them upright in a cast-iron pan, add some butter and garlic and a splash of white wine, and then cook them over a smoldering fire, with the pine needles flaming on top of them. And along with the pine needles, you can add dried rosemary and fennel branches and let those aromatics flavor your mussels as well. It never fails to wow.

Note: You can rinse pine needles and then lay them out to dry if you're worried about cleanliness. Also: DO NOT MAKE THIS INDOORS. I shouldn't even have to write that. JUST DON'T. Make it at the beach, where it can't catch anything else on fire. Have a bucket of sand and plenty of water nearby.

Build a fire. If the firepit has a grill, then the fire can still be flaming. (If not, let it burn down to glowing charcoals and put your pan directly onto the fire.)

In a large cast-iron pan, line the mussels, lips up in a circular pattern, and fill the pan with as many as possible so they stay upright.

Tuck the butter and garlic in around the mussels and pour in the white wine.

Cover with the pine needles and rosemary, if using. (Ashes of pine needles are part of the final flavor.)

Place the pan of mussels on the fire, and light the pine needles on fire. Watch it burn!

When the pine needles burn down to ashes, remove the pan from the fire.

Let people scoop mussels straight from the pan and sop up the juices with a chunk of bread torn off a baguette.

DIY: Oysters on the Half Shell

EQUIPMENT:

Shucking knife

Clean towel

Thick gloves, preferably
neoprene (optional)

Crushed ice or rock salt,
for serving

Good, fresh oysters don't really need any sauce. I understand some people might want cocktail sauce for large oysters, but this will just overwhelm the experience of small oysters the West Coast is known for. If you enjoy sauces on them, try the Rose Hip and Orange–Infused White Balsamic Vinegar on page 258 for a light, citrusy mignonette, or the delicate floral flavor of the Sakura Cherry Blossom Mignonette (recipe follows), or the sweet balance of berries and white wine vinegar in the Wild Berry Mignonette (recipes follows).

With the flat side of the oyster up, wiggle the tip of your oyster knife into the hinge.

When you hear a subtle click, twist your shucker to loosen the top of the oyster.

Run the shucker along the top of the oyster as you pry it off.

Try not to spill the oyster "liquor" (liquid inside the shell).

Clean any grit along the edge with your shucker.

Use the shucker to detach the muscle from the bottom of the oyster.

To serve, place oysters on something that will hold them upright so their liquor doesn't spill out. This can be crushed ice if setting out for an occasion, salt if you're putting them back into the fridge for a short period of time, cold seaweed à la France (with lemon wedge and mignonette), or crumbled aluminum foil works if you plan on baking them.

¼ cup champagne vinegar

1 teaspoon finely minced shallot

1 teaspoon minced Preserved Sakura Cherry Blossoms (page 264), plus a few whole petals for garnish

SAKURA CHERRY BLOSSOM MIGNONETTE

This mignonette has the tart, floral flavor of the cherry blossoms balanced with the shallots. Don't go overboard with the blossoms, though, as they are salty, and the oyster is already salty. It's just an accent.

———————————————

Combine all the ingredients in a jar with a lid and shake until incorporated or mix them in a small bowl.

If possible, chill for 30 minutes before using.

Just before serving, put in a small bowl, add a few cherry blossom petals and a few drops of the ume vinegar they soaked in for added floral flavor.

Serve alongside the oyster platter.

If not using right away, keep in a covered container and refrigerate for up to a month.

MAKES ½ CUP

¼ cup white wine vinegar

1 teaspoon finely minced shallot

2 tablespoons tart berries, such as any combination of black currants, blackberries, salmonberries

WILD BERRY MIGNONETTE

This just happened once at Wild Food Camp. Someone put berries in the mignonette sauce, and it turned out to be delicious. Wild berries are more tart than cultivated ones, so it had tannins from currants and lots of fruity notes from the other berries.

———————————————

Combine all the ingredients in a jar with a lid and shake until the berries start to break apart in the vinegar.

Chill for 30 minutes.

Put in a small bowl and serve with the oyster platter right away or keep refrigerated in a tightly lidded container for up to a month.

Aphrodite's Truffle-Butter-Baked Oysters

MAKES 12 OYSTERS

12 oysters, shucked

2 cups coarse salt, divided

½ teaspoon Compound Truffle Butter (recipe follows) per oyster

A recipe for oysters with warm truffle cream dates to the fourth century BC, as both oysters and truffles were favorites of Aphrodite, the Greek goddess of love, beauty, sex, and fertility. Both the oyster and the truffle are still considered aphrodisiacs, and they're regenerative foods from the wild and vital parts of healthy ecosystems.

While this dish is deeply luxurious, I think of it as sexy soul food. I like to make a simple version of this ancient recipe, which is basically baking oysters with truffle butter.

———————————————————————

Preheat the broiler.

Prepare your oysters just prior to serving them.

Place 1 cup of the coarse salt on a baking dish, or crumple aluminum foil so it holds the oysters in place.

Open the oysters and nestle them into the salt or foil.

Place ½ teaspoon of butter onto each one.

Put oysters under the broiler for about 1 minute. The butter should be melted and the oysters still plump and juicy, but no longer raw.

Plate on the remaining 1 cup coarse salt using tongs and serve while warm, but not too hot to the touch. ——→

1 stick salted butter
(½ cup)

1 tablespoon truffle bits
and pieces, shaved
or cut as finely as
possible

COMPOUND TRUFFLE BUTTER

When I have leftover ends and odds of truffles (I do have a truffle dog, after all!), I'll grate them into butter and freeze to preserve them.

Soften the butter by letting it sit out in a bowl for an hour or so. Mix in the truffle pieces.

Spoon the mixture into a ramekin, cover, and refrigerate, where it will keep for 30 days. Or using plastic wrap, roll into a log and freeze.

CRAB

Along the West Coast, recreational crabbing season is a time of beach parties, bonfires, and big gatherings of people bibbing up and cracking and slurping away. Dungeness and rock crabs are sustainable due to three main components, or the Three S's: Sex, Size, and Season. Females are thrown back, along with males under 6¼ inches wide. As well, Dungeness shed their shells, or molt, at different times of the year, which makes them delicate and susceptible to injury, so they aren't caught during molting season. Another element that makes them sustainable is they are caught with baited traps or hoop nets. These are designed to let smaller crabs and bycatch escape unharmed. Bycatch includes other creatures found in the traps that you were not hoping for.

Despite this, it's not free of controversy. In California commercial crabbing grounds, humpback whales are getting entangled with the long lines the baited pots are attached to. This is being addressed by biologists and commercial fishermen who are learning more about whale migration by flying over the crabbing grounds and waiting until whales have moved on before commercial crabbing begins.

New technology is being developed so fishers can use pots that aren't on lines. And crabbing gear hasn't gotten more deadly, rather, whale populations have rebounded to almost historic levels.

Before a global moratorium on commercial whaling, humpbacks were hunted to near extinction. They were used for everything from oil for the streetlights in San Francisco to hair pomade. The last whaling station in America was at Point San Pablo on the San Francisco Bay, which operated until 1971. There, they turned humpbacks into oil, poultry meal, and pet food—branded as Moby Dick, Whale Meat for Pets. There has been an international moratorium on whaling since 1985, and many populations, including the humpback that migrates along our coast, have rebounded. They now number over twenty thousand! So when you drop your crab pots or hoops, stay with them and monitor them closely so they don't drift out with a tide and injure a sea creature.

How to Catch Crab

Recreational crabbing is a much-loved autumn tradition in the SF Bay Area. It's open during windows in the summer and winter on the Puget Sound—check with Fish and Wildlife on the exact dates; some areas in Oregon are open to recreational crabbing all year. Southeast Alaska allows recreational crabbing, but the areas around Anchorage are closed to it. So always check on the rules and regulations first.

Three different types of crab traps are used for recreational crabbing. There's a crab hoop net with mesh or you can use a cage. And some people cast from shore using a fishing pole with a sort of plastic puzzle that works as a snare. All of them should have a bait box in the center. These can be attached with zip ties. Throughout the year, save fish heads, bones, guts, or any other part that might usually be thrown away. Keep them in the freezer and take them out to bait your crab pot. Chicken and turkey necks, squid, and small baitfish like anchovy work well also. (Though some anchovies may be too small and slip out of the bait box.)

Make sure your bait box is secured before tossing your cage into the water. When Dungeness crab season opens along the West Coast, people skiff, row, and paddle in kayaks and even stand-up paddleboards (SUPs) to drop their pots and hoop nets. These sit on the sea bottom, and a line attaches them to a buoy on the surface of the water.

Be sure to check the weather! You'll want to know if the tide is coming or going and if the seas will be rough. If so, wait until another day.

Dungeness Crab Boil

*MAKES 4 TO 8
SERVINGS*

¼ cup kosher salt

2 bay leaves

4 Dungeness crabs

1 cup Seaweed Aioli
(recipe follows) or
unsalted butter,
melted, for serving

1 lemon, cut into
wedges, for serving

Note: Traditionally,
a crab feed in San
Francisco means
boiled crab served
with green salad
and sourdough
baguettes. Only
suckers fill up on
the bread.

During Dungeness season, crabs are readily available at the seafood counters of grocery stores. But I like to get crabs live, preferably catch them myself, and boil them. I'm not a masochist. I want the connection to the ocean I have when checking the tides and looking for good crabbing spots. I like to know they are fresh. And I use the water seasoned from boiling the crabs to cook accompaniments to the crabs. There's a lot you can do with a big boiling pot of water, particularly if it's been flavored with crab. Toss some artichokes and new potatoes in there. You can also use the crab water to boil pasta and make a delicious *cacio e pepe* as a side dish.

Bring a large stockpot filled with salted water to a high boil.

Add the bay leaves.

Using tongs, add as many crabs as can fit into the pot without crowding them.

Cover, return to a boil, and cook the crabs for 10 minutes, until they're bright red, or about 7 minutes per pound.

Remove from the pot and let the crabs cool before cleaning them.

If serving with drawn butter, place the butter in a small saucepan over medium heat and bring to a boil.

Cook for about 1 minute, removing from the heat before it starts to turn brown.

Let stand for 5 minutes.

Skim the foam off the top of the butter, then carefully pour the yellow liquid into ramekins for serving, leaving the foam behind.

Place the boiled crab belly side up. Pull off the triangular-shaped belly apron. Remove the entire shell. Clean out the gills. Break in half.

Cut or pull off one leg at a time with part of the body attached.

Serve with lemon wedges and the butter or the Seaweed Aioli—or both.

*MAKES ABOUT
1½ CUPS*

⅔ cup avocado or other neutral oil

⅓ cup extra-virgin olive oil

Pinch of kosher salt

1 garlic clove

1 egg yolk

1 tbsp lemon juice

1 teaspoon seaweed granules (either grind your seaweed in a spice grinder or buy at the store or online; if I'm purchasing it, I like Daybreak Seaweed)

SEAWEED AIOLI

Aioli is delicious with just about anything, and fresh Dungeness crab is no exception. Added seaweed keeps it on theme for the crab's intertidal zone habitat.

Bonus points for using roasted garlic cloves.

In a small bowl or medium measuring cup, combine the oils.

In a separate small bowl, sprinkle the salt on the garlic and mash into a paste. Then add the egg yolk and lemon juice and mix.

In another bowl, using a whisk or immersion blender, or in a stand blender, add the egg mixture and start slowly drizzling the oil into it as you blend. The key to not breaking the aioli is to pour the oil very slowly. I take short pauses in pouring while I blend away. Stay focused. Do not answer a text message or call.

When it has thickened to the consistency of mayonnaise and you've used all the oil, start folding in the seaweed and continue to blend slowly until it's mixed throughout. Then cover and refrigerate. The seaweed will continue to infuse the aioli, so I suggest you use it within a week or so.

SPOT PRAWNS

Recreational spot prawn season in Washington is a tight window; for one to five days a year they are most commonly found in Hood Canal, the San Juan Islands, and northern and central Puget Sound. British Columbia and Alaska also allow limited sport spot prawn fishing with pots. In Oregon and California, the prawns are too deep for recreational fishing—and only a very small number of commercial permits are allowed to fish for them, so they tend to be very expensive. Along with a limited number of days, there's also usually a time limit—so you may drop your pots at 9:00 a.m. and have to pull them by 1:00 p.m. Check regulations carefully.

You'll most likely need to boat, dinghy, kayak, or SUP to the spot where you want to drop your pots. And it may take a while to learn your spots, so be patient and enjoy the journey. As with crabbing, you'll need a baited pot attached to a line with a buoy on it that marks your spot. There will also be a lot of hauling up your line to check your pots every hour or so.

I've asked my friend Riley Starks, a fisherman on Lummi Island, what he uses to bait his recreational spot prawn pots with. Apparently, it's a secret blend of many things that includes canned cat food. That's all I got out of him. Do with that what you will.

A note on spot prawns: When you pull them from the water, you have only a short window—maybe five hours—in which to eat them or they start to turn black. If you don't plan on cooking them right away, then pinch their heads off and store them in the fridge or on ice. Once their heads are off, they can also be frozen.

Rosemary-Salt Cooked Spot Prawns

MAKES 4 SERVINGS

6 to 8 stalks of fresh rosemary

3 pounds coarse kosher salt

16 medium to large spot prawns

My friend Riley Starks of Nettles Farm on Lummi Island has a favorite way of cooking the spot prawns he catches. He heats coarse salt mixed with freshly harvested rosemary, then pours the hot herbaceous salt over the prawns and cooks them in very high heat over an open fire. The night we ate them at Wild Food Camp, we dumped the pot of hot salt and prawns on a big platter and then shook prawns loose from the salt—this method does not form a salt crust. We simply peeled and ate them, standing around the fire. It was sublime.

VARIATION: MAKE IT OVER AN OPEN FIRE

To make this recipe outdoors, put the rosemary salt in a cast-iron pot and place in a fire that has cooked down to red-hot coals. Heat, stirring, for about 30 minutes, then add the spot prawns and mix to combine. Leave the prawns in the salt for about 6 minutes, or until the prawns are opaque. Peel and enjoy.

Preheat the oven to 400 degrees F.

Remove the rosemary leaves from the stalks and roughly chop them.

In a large bowl, add the chopped rosemary to the salt and mix to combine.

In a cast-iron pot, add the rosemary salt and put it into the oven.

Remove any roe from the spot prawns and use separately (I serve on sour cream with good potato chips).

Heat the salt for about 30 minutes, stirring on occasion to make sure it all gets very hot.

Bury the spot prawns in the hot salt and return the cast-iron pan to the oven for 6 minutes.

Remove a prawn from the pan and shake the salt off to test doneness. Prawns are fully cooked when they are opaque.

If the prawns are done, let your guests pick them from the hot salt, then peel and enjoy. Or you can remove them with tongs and plate them.

Seduction-Worthy Spot Prawns with Seaweed Aioli

MAKES 2 SERVINGS

2 tablespoons salted butter

6 to 8 medium to large spot prawns

½ cup Seaweed Aioli (page 53)

Though spot prawns are fleeting (and expensive if store-bought), they are worth it. Since they're large, buttery, and rich, the experience of eating spot prawns is more like eating lobster tails than shrimp. If you've met someone you are certain you'd like to seduce, then live-firing spot prawns will most likely close the deal—prepare the prawns on a beach as the sun fades into the Pacific. Spot prawns are too rare and wonderful to be shared with anyone not seduction-worthy.

Build a campfire somewhere with a great view. Let the wood burn down to a low flame, just before coals. Either use a campfire grate or place rocks in a circle that the cast-iron pan can sit on and be level.

In the cast-iron skillet, add the butter. When it melts down, add the spot prawns.

Cook for about 20 seconds, then flip the prawns over. They should be bright pink. They only need about 30 seconds on each side. Don't overcook them!

After 30 seconds on the other side, check their color. If pink, remove from the fire.

Serve with the aioli. Peel and eat with your hands.

Make out (optional).

UNI AND KELP SUPERHIGHWAY

Floating bulbs with long, flowing fronds bobble in frothy seas of the West Coast. This is bull kelp, an annual alga species. Under normal conditions, it releases spores in late summer and fall—prior to the arrival of winter storm waves that rip out much of the mature kelp. The following spring, spores grow rapidly in the nutrient-rich, cold waters along the Pacific coast, forming kelp forests that shelter and feed a whole host of other marine life, from rockfish to anchovies and young salmon, sea urchins, abalone, sea otters, sea stars, and kelp bass.

There's a theory that the first people to migrate to the Americas were hunter-gatherers who came over from Siberia across the Bering Land Bridge about 13,500 years ago. They made their way from Alaska to South America along this "kelp superhighway" as it was a rich source of food.

Since 2014, the Sonoma and Mendocino coast has lost more than 90 percent of its bull kelp forest due to warming waters caused by climate change, according to a 2019 study. Due to this, abalone diving has been closed for the foreseeable future; the red abalone have been starving because of the lack of bull kelp. However, purple sea urchins have been rapidly expanding, forming massive "feeding fronts," known as urchin barrens.

The urchin population explosion has been due to a number of climate change–related factors: in 2011, there was a toxic algal bloom along the Sonoma coast that killed off many invertebrates that live in shallow waters, including huge numbers of abalone, along with sea stars, and even urchins. This set the stage for the 2013 outbreak of sea star wasting disease, which affected the West Coast from Baja to Alaska. Sea stars fed on purple urchins, so the urchin population exploded. A marine heat wave, or "warm blog," hit in 2014, then the strong El Niño of 2015 ushered in warmer waters, which have fewer nutrients than cold upwellings normal for coastal California and required for kelp growth. The urchins increased the size of their jaws and teeth, so they have access to more food, and came out of crevices and formed feeding fronts. An estimated 250 miles of these purple urchin barrens exist along the coast of northern Sonoma and Mendocino Counties. The daily limit for purple sea urchins in California is currently 35 (5–gallon) buckets. Yes, 175 gallons of purple sea urchins per person, per day.

SEA URCHINS

We are eating for a climate solution here, and fresh uni is an utter delight. These are the creamy orange roe sacks of the sea urchin. When they are right out of the ocean and the golden lobes are full, the texture is firm and silken. The flavor is reminiscent of flowing kelp and Pacific upwells. Uni served in restaurants most commonly comes from red sea urchins, which are larger than purple urchins, but there is a glut of purple urchins right now that are wreaking havoc on bull kelp ecosystems.

Purple sea urchin can be harvested year-round, but seem to be fattest from October to December. Get the ones closest to seaweed, as they will be full of uni and you're saving the seaweed from being devoured. Depending on what types of algae they are feeding on, they may have a delicate, sweet ocean flavor, or a more iodine, savory flavor. In the thick urchin barrens they will not have much, if any, uni. You can either scuba dive for sea urchins or, if legal, gather them on low tide from tide pools. Either way, you need a fishing license or permit.

Harvesting Tips

- Check your tide chart and the weather. If there are high seas, wait until it's calm. Even if you're picking in tide pools, it can be dangerous during stormy seas.

- Use gloves! These guys feel as prickly as they look. I use thick neoprene diving gloves.

- If you are harvesting from tide pools, be sure and watch where you step—avoid hurting any little sea creatures like barnacles or anemones.

- Dip your hands/gloves into seawater before touching anything in a tide pool.

- Leave the tide pool as you found it. If you move any rocks, be sure to put them back. It's probably a creature's home.

DIY: Uni on the Half Shell

EQUIPMENT:

Gloves, preferably neoprene

Scissors or garden pruners

Needle-nose pliers

Small spoon

Plastic squeeze bottle

Salt water—preferably seawater, or a 1:10 salt-to-water mixture

Super fresh and simple is the best way to enjoy uni. Find a nice flat rock and enjoy your harvest. You're helping the ocean, and eating these will light you up in all kinds of ways. If you love the texture and sensory experience of raw oysters, you'll probably be an uni fan.

After harvesting with gloves on, if you are taking the urchins to eat at home, don't clean them right away, but rather put the sea urchins in a cooler with a little ocean water and a little seaweed for them to eat. They can stay alive for a day or two that way.

To clean purple urchin, take a pair of scissors and cut around the bottom. They have a beak, so if this doesn't come out with the cut, you can pull it out with needle-nose pliers.

Shake out the guts. You should see about 5 small lobes of uni left in the shell. Clean around them with a small spoon, removing any other innards.

Fill a plastic squeeze bottle with salt water and squirt around the lobes to clean out the rest of the uni.

Eat them raw, right there out of the shell (my favorite way), or grill them over a wood fire (page 62).

Note: If you find uni that doesn't look perfect or slithers out in a gooey pile instead of a well-shaped tongue, there are lots of things you can do with it. I combine it with soft butter to make an uni-flavored compound butter. You can then freeze this in small jars and use when you'd like. Toss it with buckwheat soba noodles and garnish with gomasio for a quick meal.

Grilled Uni

MAKES 4 APPETIZERS

8 live sea urchins

1 lemon, cut into
  wedges and
  deseeded

Pinch of finishing salt

I learned this trick from Douglas Bernstein, who is amazing with seafood. He was the executive chef at Fish restaurant in Sausalito for over ten years. After a rough shift, he wanted something warm to eat, but raw uni was the only thing he could find, so he popped it on a wood-fired grill at the restaurant. It was just what he needed: delicious and warm, with a smoky essence from the wood fire.

———————————————

Clean the uni and remove them from the shell (page 61). Wash out the shell, and put the uni back into it.

Put the cleaned urchins on a grill for 3 to 4 minutes, or until you see a slight bubble and they're warm to the touch.

Squeeze some fresh lemon juice and sprinkle a little finishing salt onto each one.

Serve warm.

LITTLE FISH

Clusters of birds dive-bombing the water and breaching humpbacks are a good sign that bait balls of small fish are on the move. These could be herring, sardines, mackerel, or anchovies—critical forage fish of the ocean food web. Unfortunately, they've fallen out of fashion as a food source, and instead are commercially fished for fertilizer, feed for industrial salmon and chicken farms, and in the case of herring, they are prized for their roe only. And it takes three pounds of baitfish for one pound of farmed salmon. So why not just eat the little fish? They are delicious, nutritious powerhouses that are low in mercury and contaminants and often easy to catch from shore. Small fish are high in protein and omega-3s. They're a lot of work to clean, but well worth the effort. Anchovies have a huge and growing fan base, but there are still the haters! I think they have gotten a bad rap from uninspired pizza in many people's checkered little-fish past.

Herring can start arriving in bays in the late fall and continue deep into spring, but the peak season tends to be in January and February; whereas anchovies are in season from April through October, so chances are whenever you are looking to catch small fish, you'll be able to find some. The schools are arriving when the roars of sea lions keep you awake at night, or you wake up to clouds of pelicans, egrets, and cormorants hitting the water, seagulls squawking.

Commercial fishing of herring and other small fish has slowed in recent years because of scarce rain, warming ocean temperatures, and other changes in the ocean. And since the tradition of eating herring eggs is dying out in Japan, prices have dropped and there are no canneries in place to process herring for food, even if people did eat them.

Small fish have much more value left in the water, as they are a vital part of the food web, which humans have traditionally participated in for thousands of years. In Puget Sound, they were a central part of the diet for the Native peoples. Little fish are the drivers of a healthy ecosystem.

When I go out with my throw net to catch herring on the San Francisco Bay or a jigging rig to catch anchovies, I am very conscious that I do this as part of my surrounding ecosystem. I know that the sea lions are satisfied, and the pelicans are so full they can barely fly. I take a modest amount, about half of a five-gallon bucket, for personal use. (By comparison, commercial herring fishermen can land over ten tons in one day.) You can grill the fresh ones for dinner and invite friends over. Then fillet others and pickle them; save the egg sacs, dab them into olive oil, and pack them into salt to use as bottarga. The smelt can be dipped into flour and cooked in butter for a spread over toast. The heads and guts can be blended with ground turkey for pet food.

By eating from our local waterways, we have a vested, visceral interest in keeping them clean and healthy. Driving to the store to buy seafood imported from China or Scotland illustrates our disconnect from nature. It's turning our backs on our waterways. Get a throw net or a herring jig, and follow the frenzy of birds and seals to baitfish.

How to Catch Small Fish

When you hear the sea lions bellowing and see pelicans and cormorants take to the skies, tufts of light and darkness that dive-bomb the water, the herring are arriving. They travel in schools that historically were massive. Now, they are more like pulses, making their way to beds of eelgrass, where they lay their eggs. Grab your throw net or your jig setup and head to the action. Along the San Francisco Bay, there are many places where you can catch them from shore—downtown Sausalito is one of the hot spots. In Oregon, check Tillamook Bay, Coos Bay, Winchester Bay, and Yaquina Bay. For the Salish Sea, the Strait of Georgia has the last abundant herring run. (The Conservancy Hornby Island has a HerringFest each spring where you can witness the natural spectacle of herring arriving. There's also an annual Herring Fest in Sausalito.)

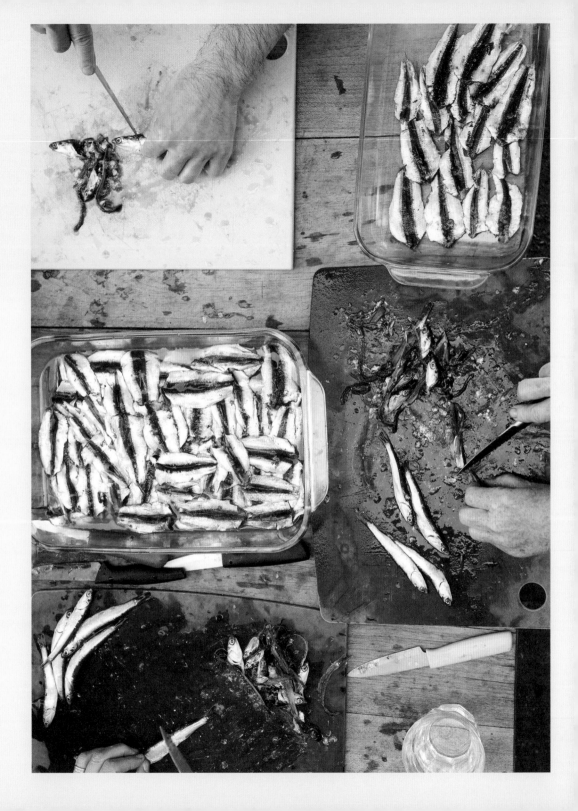

Grilled Herring

MAKES 4 SERVINGS

20 whole fresh herring (or sardines or mackerel), cleaned, gilled, and gutted

2 tablespoons extra-virgin olive oil

Sea salt

Freshly ground black pepper

Peels of an entire preserved lemon (page 212), cut into slivers, or 2 lemons, halved and deseeded

If you're grilling a herring—or sardine or mackerel—you don't need to fillet them. Using your knife, gently scrape the scales from them. Then simply run your knife down the belly, but not so deeply that you'd damage an egg sac. Remove the guts and discard. If you find an egg sac, it will be translucent yellow with faint blood vessels; remove and set aside to cure for bottarga (page 70). Remove the gill just behind the head.

———————————————————

Set the grill to 400 degrees F.

In a large bowl, toss the fish with the oil, salt, and pepper.

Grill about 3 minutes per side, or until the skin starts to char.

Serve with the lemon peels or halves.

Spaghetti with Herring Bottarga, Orange Zest, Ricotta, and Fresh Herbs

MAKES 6 TO 8 SERVINGS

2 cups ricotta

2 tablespoons fresh marjoram or thyme leaves

Zest of 2 sweet oranges (like Valencia or navel)

1 pound dry spaghetti

5 egg sacs from Salt-Preserved Herring Bottarga (recipe follows), cut into the thinnest slivers possible

1 teaspoon kosher salt

1 teaspoon freshly cracked black pepper

Chopped parsley, for garnish

Note: For extra umami flavor, use the Seaweed Pasta (page 21) instead of plain spaghetti.

If convincing people to eat herring is difficult, imagine selling them on making a meal of herring eggs. Traditionally, *pasta con la bottarga* is a simple (and thrifty) regional Italian dish using either mullet or tuna eggs that have been dried and salt-preserved. When I was talking with local Italian chef Viola Buitoni, she unlocked a whole new world to me. "Bottarga is excellent with oranges," she sagely told me. This shouldn't have been such a shock since I used citrus to pickle herring. But still, sweet oranges with salty fish eggs? Turns out, this addition has made this recipe one of my all-time favorites.

In a large bowl, mix the ricotta, herbs, and orange zest.

Cook the pasta according to package directions.

Before draining, save 2 cups of the pasta water.

Drain and rinse the pasta.

Slowly add about 1 cup of the pasta water to the ricotta mixture to get the consistency of a thick cream sauce. Use more pasta water if needed.

Add the pasta, sliced herring bottarga, salt, and pepper to the ricotta mixture and toss until the noodles are coated.

Garnish with parsley and serve.

2 cups fine kosher salt, divided

10 herring egg sacs

2 tablespoons extra-virgin olive oil

SALT-PRESERVED HERRING BOTTARGA

I keep a container of salt-preserved fish bottarga in my fridge all year long—it lasts a long time. On occasion, I'll change out the salt as the olive oil may dampen it. You can use it in recipes that call for tinned anchovies or fish sauce—though it's milder than both of those. If you're making a green goddess dressing, just grate or shave some bottarga into it. I'll use it sparingly when I caramelize cabbage in butter and tamari, or add it to a bean stew or braised greens with lemon. In Italy, it's often grated over pasta with lemon zest and toasted bread crumbs.

———————————————

Coat the bottom of a lidded glass container (about 4 by 4 inches) with 1 cup of the salt.

Dip each of the egg sacs into the oil—this helps protect and preserve the sac.

Lay them in the salt.

Sprinkle the remaining salt over the herring sacs.

Put the lid on the container and leave in the fridge.

After a few weeks, change out the salt if it looks damp.

The bottarga will be good for a year.

Pickled Herring Board with Preserved Lemon and Sumac Crème Fraîche

MAKES 4 TOASTS

7½ ounces crème fraîche (see note)

3 tablespoons diced and mashed preserved lemon (page 212)

1 teaspoon sumac powder

½ red onion, thinly sliced

4 Blood Orange and Meyer Lemon Pickled Herring (recipe follows) fillets, cut into 2–inch pieces

1 small watermelon radish, sliced as thinly as possible with a mandoline

½ cup microgreens

Finishing salt

Freshly ground black pepper

4 slices rye bread, toasted

Pickled herring over toasted squares of rye bread with crunchy radishes, microgreens, and creamy crème fraîche is reminiscent of a classic Danish *smørrebrød*. However you serve it, pickled herring will be met with tears of joy if the person receiving it is Scandinavian, German, or Dutch, or grew up in old-school Jewish culture in New York City. Others may be skeptical, but pickled herring will win most people over quickly. You can use fresh onion for this board, but I like to use the onion pickled in the Blood Orange and Meyer Lemon Pickled Herring jars.

In a small bowl, combine the crème fraîche, preserved lemon, and sumac until just mixed.

Smear the crème fraîche mix in a shallow serving platter.

Place the onion on the crème fraîche.

Arrange the herring fillet pieces on top of the onions and crème fraîche.

Scatter the radish and microgreens over the herring, and top with salt and pepper.

Place the toast squares around the edge of the platter.

Note: If you don't have crème fraîche, plain yogurt or sour cream also works. When you use an electric blender, the crème fraîche will thin out; therefore, I recommend mixing by hand so it's thick and spreadable on the toast.

2 cups apple cider
vinegar

2 cups water

1 tablespoon sugar

1 tablespoon kosher salt

10 medium to large
whole fresh herring,
scaled, gutted, and
gilled

1 blood orange, sliced

1 Meyer lemon, sliced

1 small red onion,
thinly sliced with a
mandoline

10 pink peppercorns

2 bay laurel leaves (if
using California bay
laurel, use only 1 leaf,
as they are strongly
flavored)

BLOOD ORANGE AND MEYER LEMON PICKLED HERRING

This recipe is for traditional, old-school-style herring fillets pickled in vinegar. The citrus adds some nice notes to it, but it still goes great with sour cream, rye, and dill. I use them on boards at brunch or as appetizers, and they're great on salads; you can julienne them into coleslaw for "Glassblowers Slaw."

_____

In a saucepan on low heat, add the apple cider vinegar and water. Add the sugar and salt. Stir until the sugar and salt dissolve and are heated through. Remove from the heat and set aside to cool.

Fillet the fish by laying your fillet knife behind the gills and slicing through to the spine bone.

Twist your knife so it lies flat and run it along the bones in one cut down the length of the body. Be sure to slide the knife; don't hack or saw at it.

Flip the fish over and repeat. The second side of a fish is always harder to fillet than the first—just hold it firmly.

Into two clean 16-ounce wide-mouth mason jars, tuck your herring fillets with the scales facing the outside for aesthetics.

Tuck the orange and lemon slices between them.

Divide the onion slices, pink peppercorns, and bay laurel leaves between the jars.

Fill with the cooled pickling liquid.

Seal and refrigerate overnight before eating.

Keeps about a month in the fridge.

Fire-Roasted Steckerlfisch

MAKES 12 SKEWERS

1 cup orange juice

3 tablespoons apple cider vinegar

2 tablespoons extra-virgin olive oil

1 teaspoon kosher salt

1 teaspoon freshly ground black pepper

12 whole fresh herring (or sardines or mackerel), scaled, gutted, and gilled

12 long skewers (at least 12 inches), soaked in water for at least 3 hours

Each year, a nonprofit on the Sausalito waterfront, the Sausalito Community Boating Center, holds a Herring Festival to raise money. Former executive chef Douglas Bernstein of the local seafood restaurant Fish showed up with a big Bavarian-style grill and passed out herring on a stick. It was wildly cool and popular. But they taste even better roasted on an open fire, so this recipe is great for when you're on a camping trip. Just be sure to clean your fish by taking out the guts and gills so they will stay fresh longer. If using herring right away, you don't need to remove the gills. Douglas uses a spray bottle for the brine, but you can also brush them if you don't have a bottle handy.

———————————

Build a fire and let the wood burn down to a low flame, just before coals.

In a small bowl, mix the orange juice, vinegar, oil, salt, and pepper. Whisk together and then, using a funnel, transfer to a clean spray bottle.

Skewer the fish through the mouth and down the backbone to ensure a tight fit.

Place the skewers on the edge of the firepit at an angle over the fire, turning slightly every few minutes until the skin of the fish starts to char, 6 to 7 minutes.

As you turn the fish, spray each one with the orange mixture, making sure to shake often.

Smoked Anchovies

MAKES 10 SMOKED ANCHOVIES

2 cups wood chips (such as cherry, apple, or hickory; see note)

10 anchovies, cleaned and filleted

Note: Using hickory wood chips results in a stronger wood flavor, whereas cherry wood results in a more delicate flavor.

Smoking little fish like herring and anchovies is a great way to preserve them, and you don't even have to have a fancy smoker to do it. I've used this method on the stove top for years, until I got a *donabe* smoker. You just need a sturdy roasting pan and a grate that fits inside it. Anchovies preserved this way make a great compound butter like the Smoked Anchovy Butter on page 78; or they can be frozen, or sealed and vacuum-packed, and pulled out for dips and schmears.

_____

Preheat the oven to 350 degrees F.

In a medium bowl, soak the wood chips in water for 30 minutes.

Cover the bottom of a deep roasting pan with foil and spread the damp wood chips over the foil.

Place a grate in the pan over the wood chips.

Lay the fish on the grate, skin side down, and cover the whole roasting pan with foil.

Cook in the oven for 8 to 12 minutes, or until the fish is soft but not falling apart.

Remove from the heat and cool.

MAKES SLIGHTLY
OVER ½ CUP OF
BUTTER, ABOUT 10
TABLESPOONS

**½ cup unsalted butter,
room temperature**

**8 medium smoked
anchovies (page 77)**

**½ teaspoon fresh thyme
leaves**

**½ teaspoon chopped
fresh basil leaves**

¼ teaspoon kosher salt

SMOKED ANCHOVY BUTTER

This too you can make with just about any of the little fish. Herring is excellent smoked and can be creamed into butter. You can serve this alongside bread or toss noodles in it. I like it with the seaweed pasta. It's also wonderful over a grilled piece of beef or black cod.

In a medium bowl, mash by hand the butter and anchovies until thoroughly creamed.

Add the fresh herbs and salt and mix until combined.

Use right away, or store covered in the fridge for up to a week. Alternatively, freeze and then thaw before using.

Panko-Fried Anchovies with Crispy Nori Seaweed

MAKES 4 SERVINGS

1 cup flour

1 teaspoon kosher salt

½ teaspoon freshly ground black pepper

½ teaspoon red chili flakes

2 large eggs, lightly beaten

2 cups panko

Avocado oil or other high-heat oil, for frying

20 anchovies, cleaned and filleted

8 sheets nori, torn in 2-by-2-inch pieces

1 lemon, halved and cut into thin half-moon slivers

Seaweed Gomasio (page 83), for garnish

These are really delicious. Fresh anchovies are astonishingly light in flavor and texture and are enhanced with a little crunch and a dipping sauce. People go crazy for these. You just want to make sure and work quickly so they're served while still warm. They lose a bit of their magic if they cool down. These fillets can be served with an aioli or ponzu dipping sauce, or just a squeeze of lemon.

In a large shallow dish, combine the flour, salt, pepper, and chili flakes.

Place the eggs and panko in two separate shallow dishes. Set aside, but keep nearby the stove.

In a deep skillet over medium-high heat, add 1 inch of the oil.

Dredge the anchovies in the flour, egg, and then panko.

Fry the anchovies in the hot oil in a single layer until golden brown.

Remove with a slotted spoon and lay on a plate lined with paper towels.

With a slotted spoon, remove the bits of panko in the oil and then repeat dredging and frying with the nori. It will get soggy, so work quickly! And then repeat the process with the lemon slices.

Remove all from the oil and let drain on plates lined with paper towels, and then plate and sprinkle with the gomasio.

Lemony Salt-Preserved Anchovies

*MAKES TWO
8-OUNCE JARS, OR
FOUR 4-OUNCE JARS*

20 anchovies, cleaned
  and filleted

½ cup kosher salt

2 cups fresh lemon juice

2 cups extra-virgin olive
  oil, divided

2 garlic cloves
  (optional)

2 lemon slices (optional)

10 peppercorns
  (optional)

Always keep your seafood on ice, but particularly the little fish. So have ice in your cooler and on your workstation and store your fish in the fridge as you go. When I make this, I get probably 75 to 120 little fish, which is way too many to fillet by myself, so I pre-organize an "Anchovy Olympics," where a group of my friends come together to fillet anchovies and juice lemons. I play music and make snacks and demonstrate how to fillet. Everyone leaves with jars of these delicious little fish. Use them on crostini, over salads, mixed with sautéed greens, or just eat them from the jar. I like to serve them on seaweed bread with seaweed butter in an Intertidal Zone Grazing Board (page 85).

_____

Lay the anchovy fillets flat on a baking sheet. Sprinkle them with the salt evenly and put in the fridge for 20 minutes.

Remove from the fridge and rinse.

In a large, deep dish, pour the lemon juice over the fillets. Make sure they are all submerged. Put them in the fridge for at least an hour.

Remove and taste. The fillets should be firm and salty, but not too salty and not too lemony. The essence of the anchovy should always be there. When it's the texture and flavor you like, remove from the lemon juice.

Place them evenly in two clean, small glass jars with the skin side facing out for aesthetics.

Fill each jar with the oil. Add the aromatics, the garlic cloves, lemon slices, and peppercorns, to each jar.

Seal the jars and store in the fridge for up to 6 months.

DIY: Making Sea Salt

MAKES ABOUT 4 CUPS

1 to 2 wide-mouth 5-gallon buckets with lids

Large pot

Cheesecloth

2 to 3 large baking pans

I have known and loved many bays and coastlines. Some have been long-term relationships, others shorter yet passionate affairs, but I wish I had a jar of salt from each of them. Homemade salt can have a marvelous *merroir*, or sense of a particular coast. It's a way to freeze in time a memory of a place that's in constant flux and motion.

Harvesting salt can be as simple as stomping into the ocean with a bucket in hand, or as tricky as balancing on a slippery rock while trying to scoop up a wave crashing near you. The ocean can catch you by surprise, so keep safety first. You also want to be sure and harvest water far away from large urban areas, farms, or anywhere that might be polluted.

―――――――――――――――

Collect seawater in your bucket, then secure the water with a snugly fitting lid to transport it.

Let it sit for a day or so, allowing the sediment to settle to the bottom. Pour the water into a second bucket or stockpot, leaving behind the sediment in the original bucket. Pour this water through a cheesecloth once or twice to strain out any debris.

In a large pot over high heat, boil the seawater down until half the water has evaporated, about 3 hours. Stir well and then simmer for another 4 to 6 hours. Don't let it scorch!

When it gets to a wet-cement consistency, spread the salt out into baking pans and let it air-dry, or pop it into the oven on the lowest-possible temperature until it is dry and flaky, scraping the sides with a spatula every so often to loosen it. You can grind it into a fine powder-like salt with a spice grinder if you like, or leave it in chunky flakes.

Once it's dry, store in a clean glass jar and label.

¼ cup seaweed
granules

¾ cup flaky sea salt

SEAWEED SALT

Use this minerally salt for finishing on savory foods, or for adding a touch of salty crunch to brownies, cookies, or caramels.

_____

Blend seaweed granules with the salt.

½ cup toasted black
sesame seeds

½ cup toasted white
sesame seeds

⅛ cup minced seaweed
blend of kombu, nori,
and sea lettuce

⅛ cup flaky sea salt

SEAWEED GOMASIO

Gomasio is a tasty and healthy condiment originally from Japan that can be used on anything you'd usually salt. It adds a nutty, crunchy flavor to poached eggs, sweet potatoes, and soba noodles, which are my go-tos.

_____

In a small bowl, combine all the ingredients. I like to give them a whirl or two in the spice blender so they don't separate into their own factions.

Transfer to a small jar. Keeps up to a year, but taste to make sure the sesame seeds aren't getting stale.

VARIATION: SPICY TOGARASHI

_____

To make something with a little more spice, like a _togarashi_, add ⅛ teaspoon of dried orange zest, ⅛ teaspoon of red chili flakes, and ⅛ teaspoon of ground Szechuan peppercorns to the Seaweed Gomasio. Adjust all the spices according to your preference.

INTERTIDAL ZONE GRAZING BOARD

Seaweed, Seed, Oat, and Nut Bread (page 13)
with Seaweed Butter (page 28) and Lemony
Salt-Preserved Anchovies (page 80)

Fire-Roasted Butter Clams with Seaweed
Gremolata (page 36)

Blood Orange and Meyer Lemon
Pickled Herring (page 72)

Seaweed Aioli (page 53) with crudités

Oysters on the Half Shell (page 45)
with Sakura Cherry Blossom Mignonette (page 46)

THE

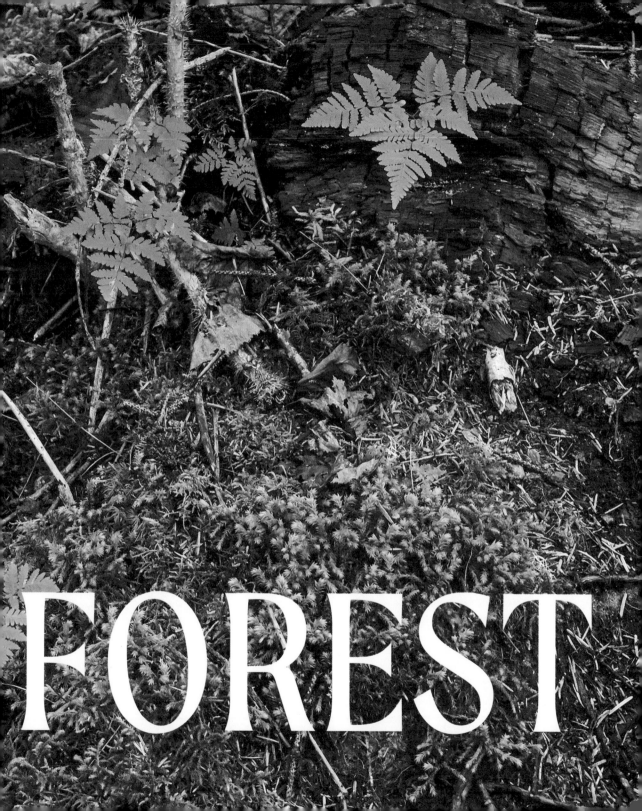

FOREST

Trees are "social creatures" that communicate with each other in cooperative ways that hold lessons for humans, too.

—SUZANNE SIMARD, *FINDING THE MOTHER TREE*

~~~~~~~~~~~~~~~~

FOREST GEAR LIST

- Brimmed hat (to stop falling creatures and protect from sun and rain)
- Long socks (to protect from scratches, scrapes, and poison oak)
- Long pants and long-sleeved shirts
- Sturdy boots with ankle support (so you don't roll your ankles on uneven ground or a log)
- Tecnu Outdoor Skin Cleanser (to wash up if you encounter thickets of poison oak)
- Bug spray (such as lemon-eucalyptus oil)
- Porcini knife (for cutting and cleaning mushrooms)
- Compass or navigational app (if an app, make sure it can be used off-line)
- Drinking water and snacks for you and canine and feline companions (yes, I've seen a mushroom hunter with his cat; I don't know him, but I admire him)
- Basket or backpack

When learning to hunt mushrooms, you must first learn about trees. Even when it's dry and not yet mushroom season, when you walk in the woods, take note. Douglas fir about thirty to fifty years old, with trunks you could wrap your arms around, are prime habitat for the Oregon white and Oregon black truffle, matsutake grow with manzanita and tan oaks, pines for the porcini and oak trees for chanterelles, and polypores like oyster mushrooms can grow on many types of trees. The more you hike in the woods, the more you'll notice the exquisite beauty of moss and lichen growing on dead branches. The rotting logs in a dilatory tumble down the streams. Ferns springing from bog-like muck. Small caverns of mold and rot under fallen trees, a perfect spiderweb guarding an entrance. You start to enter into their world.

While out learning the woods for mushrooms, I collect other edibles from this ecosystem. It's exciting to see the pale-green tips appear on pines and firs, to gather California bay laurel nuts and leaves and notice the ferns start to break ground in the spring. After spending time in the woods, it makes sense to use pine nuts and needles on a flatbread with black trumpets, to have a grazing platter with mushroom pâté and pickled fiddlehead ferns, for dessert after porcini risotto at a campfire to be bay laurel nut cacao. The forest shows us what goes well together.

Mushrooms

MUSHROOMS ARE NOT SOLITARY, BUT RATHER the fruiting bodies of mycelium, a complex underground web. Under a single footstep, there can be four hundred miles of fungal networks creating healthier and more robust forest ecosystems.

Mycologist Paul Stamets wrote, "I want to redefine Darwinian theory. It is not the survival of the fittest. It is the extension of generosity, of surplus to other members in the ecological community to build biodiversity. So it's not the individual that survives, it's the community that cooperates that survives." Mushrooms teach us how to thrive as a beneficial part of a bigger ecosystem.

The more you venture into the forest, the more you'll start to see which plants certain mushrooms grow next to. You don't go out and look for mushrooms, you look for habitat. When you find mushrooms, note the altitudes, and days after a significant rainfall, and the direction it is facing. There are often more nearby on the same root system, and you then have the opportunity to contribute to their propagation. If mushrooms are the fruit, then spores are the seeds. They benefit from being spread, so some recreational foragers use baskets, which also keep the mushrooms more pristine than a bag and help spores scatter.

Often, you will return home with a mixed bag of edible mushrooms. They may not be enough on their own for any single-mushroom recipe, but you can combine them to make layered, deeply savory dishes. The recipes in the beginning of this chapter call for a hodgepodge of wild mushrooms.

Layering mushrooms like chanterelles, black trumpets, and hedgehogs just makes for something truly magical. Add a little porcini powder or some dried morels to a pot of something savory stewing, and the effect is alchemical.

MUSHROOM IDENTIFICATION AND SAFETY

In terms of eating mushrooms, of the thousands of different ones, there is a spectrum that runs from delicious to deadly. The delicious and the deadly are only a fraction of the population. Most fungi you find in forests either don't taste very good or might give you gastric distress. But porcini, chanterelles, black trumpets, candy caps, oyster, and morels are so, so delicious. And the deadly ones are merciless. If you ingest an *Amanita phalloides*, or death cap, it's a three-day hideously painful death march. So DO NOT EVER eat a mushroom if you aren't 150 percent sure what it is.

I chose to learn culinary mushrooms one by one, so I was entirely certain of anything I put into my mouth. And I chose to not include any mushrooms in the *Amanita* genus in this book, so that nobody who reads this goes out and makes a deadly mistake. Some *Amanitas* are delicious and safe, but they are not for beginner mushroomers. When you're starting out, I urge you to never eat a mushroom that is not ID'd by an expert. One way to learn more is to join a local mycological club. You can also use apps, find social media groups, and reach out to people who have been mushroom hunting for a long time. One benefit to learning them slowly and thoroughly is not only living a longer life with your internal organs intact but also getting really proficient in the ways of preparing them. Not just the different species, but you will learn how to prepare mushrooms as they age—from young and perfect to a bit worn and soggy or wormholed—which happens quickly in the life of a mushroom. I'd rather know a few mushrooms very well than hundreds I'm iffy on.

BEST PRACTICES FOR HARVESTING MUSHROOMS

1 Tread lightly. Be mindful of damaging the forest ecosystem—stay on established trails when possible. Mycelium has a symbiotic relationship with the roots of trees. There's a vast system of communication that takes place in forests through mycorrhizal networks. So while you can't overharvest mushrooms, foragers can do damage to the forest floors.

2 Pick clean. Clean your mushrooms on the spot by scraping the dirt off the base and dusting the caps. The scrapings will help bring them back in future years and will also serve to hide the evidence of your harvest. Mushroom hunting can be very competitive. Don't let others know your spots.

3 Respect. I'm not sure why it bothers me so much when I go down a path and see people have kicked and stomped mushrooms for no reason. This doesn't hurt the mycelium, but still: please don't be that person. Even if mushrooms aren't edible, they may still be beautiful or interesting, and they play an important role in an ecosystem.

STAGES OF A MUSHROOM'S LIFE

AGE & DESCRIPTION	BEST RECIPES	STORING
What the pros look for: young, moderately sized, pristine, clear in color without bugs or mushy spots.	Use in simple recipes so they really shine.	Store in a paper bag or laid out on paper towels in the fridge for up to a week or even two.
Recreational picker's favorites: big, photogenic, firm, free from wormholes.	Due to larger size, these can be the center-of-the-plate dishes.	Store in a paper bag or on paper towels in the fridge and use within three to four days.
A little past their prime: cosmetically challenged, perhaps a little soggy.	Use for broths, seasoning, and dried and ground to mix with salt.	Will last in the fridge for maybe two days.
Leave it in the ground—it's already a biodegrading worm condo, so note the location and make it there earlier the next year.		

BLACK TRUMPET

CHANTERELLE

CANDY CAP

HEDGEHOG

Mushroom "Bone" Broth

10 cups water

2 cups wild mushroom bits, or 1½ cups dried mushrooms

½ large yellow onion, roughly chopped (about 1 cup)

2 pieces of kombu seaweed (optional)

2 large garlic cloves, roughly chopped

2 inches fresh ginger, unpeeled, scrubbed, and roughly chopped

1 tablespoon sea salt

1 teaspoon freshly ground black pepper

½ teaspoon red chili flakes (optional)

Small bundle of fresh herbs (like thyme, rosemary, bay leaf)

I try to save my vegetable waste: the green parts of leeks, ginger scrapings, the herb stalks, tips and ends of carrots, celery, kohlrabi—you name it, I keep in a lidded container in my fridge. Then I add it to water along with the various wild mushroom bits—the tips or stems or spongy pores of boletes you would normally throw away—for broth. I might also add a few pieces of seaweed or medicinal mushrooms like reishi and turkey tail to this broth. I make this once a week and use it as a basis for many dishes—like soups and risotto, to poach eggs, cook beans, and braise vegetables. It's delicious and nutritious, a great way to get the nutrients from your produce that would usually go to waste.

In a large pot over medium to high heat, add all the ingredients and bring to a boil for about 5 minutes. Then simmer on low for 30 minutes.

Strain the broth and when cool, store in the fridge for up to 2 weeks.

Creamy Sunchoke and Wild Mushroom Soup

MAKES 4 APPETIZERS SERVINGS OR 2 MAIN COURSES

3 cups Mushroom "Bone" Broth (page 96)

4 tablespoons unsalted butter, divided

½ large yellow onion, diced (about 1 cup)

3 medium sunchokes, finely diced (about 1 ½ cups)

2 garlic cloves, minced

3 cups mixed mushrooms, diced

1 teaspoon kosher salt

1 teaspoon freshly ground black pepper

1 teaspoon fresh rosemary, minced

½ teaspoon Urfa chili or red chili flakes

1 cup heavy cream

2 tablespoons tapioca pearls

4 tablespoons water, room temperature

One of the most challenging parts of hosting a gathering is getting all the dietary restrictions accommodated in one dish. For a winter gathering, I had vegetarians, a gluten-free guest, and a keto friend in the house. So I came up with this soup. I used sunchokes instead of potatoes since they are lower on the glycemic index for people following keto-ish diets. It could easily be vegan by substituting nondairy cream. Adding tapioca toward the end gives it a thicker, silky texture. This soup is just perfect when coming in from mushroom hunting on a winter day! It can be easily doubled to feed more people.

_____

In a medium stockpot over low heat, add the mushroom broth.

Melt 3 tablespoons of the butter in a sauté pan and add the onions. Sauté until translucent. Stir in the sunchokes and garlic. Sauté until the sunchokes are just about cooked through, 3 to 5 minutes. They will be tender but still somewhat crisp and will not fall apart like potatoes.

Add the mushrooms and the remaining tablespoon of butter. Stir and add the salt, pepper, rosemary, and Urfa chili.

Add the mushroom mixture to the mushroom broth and cook on medium-low heat for 10 minutes. Stir in the cream and allow to heat through.

In a small bowl, mix the tapioca with the water. Add to the soup, continuing to stir. Simmer on low for another 5 to 10 minutes.

Divide into bowls and serve.

Herby Mushroom Leek Toasts

MAKES 4 SERVINGS

3 tablespoons salted butter

1 cup chopped leeks

3 cups chopped wild mushrooms (see note)

1 teaspoon kosher salt

½ teaspoon freshly ground black pepper

½ teaspoon finely chopped fresh herbs (like rosemary, thyme, or sage)

4 slices ¼-inch-thick sourdough bread, toasted

⅓ cup shaved Parmesan

Mushrooms sautéed with leek (or onion or shallot) in butter with salt is so simple and adapts to a variety of dishes. I'll use mushrooms like this over Cedar-Planked Black Cod (page 114), tossed with pasta, on flatbreads and polenta—you can add a splash of red wine and make a sauce for pork tenderloin. But my favorite go-to vehicle for wild mushrooms is toasted artisanal sourdough bread. It lets the mushroom flavors shine and works for any culinary mushroom. Make this over a campfire, as appetizers for a party, or if you want it for breakfast, just add an egg.

In a large pan over medium-high heat, melt the butter and add the leeks. Sauté until translucent.

Add the mushrooms, salt, pepper, and herbs and cook until everything is browned, 6 to 7 minutes.

Plate the toasts, pile mushrooms on top, and garnish with the Parmesan.

Note: You can use any culinary mushroom for this. Just keep in mind if you're using chanterelles or any other mushrooms that absorb a lot of water, you'll want to dry-cook them first to get the water out. And if using black trumpets or yellowfoot chanterelles, no need to chop them if they're small.

Mushroom Pâté with Wine-Soaked Walnuts

MAKES 3 CUPS

½ cup walnuts

1 cup red wine

3 tablespoons salted butter

1 small shallot, finely diced

2 cups mixed mushrooms, chopped

3 cloves roasted garlic, or 2 cloves raw garlic

½ teaspoon fresh thyme

Kosher salt

Freshly ground black pepper

Using a variety of mushrooms in this pâté gives it more depth. So if you come back with a chanterelle that got torn up in your bag, a smattering of hedgehogs, a lone oyster mushroom, mushroom bits and pieces in the bottom of your foraging basket, or have a few shiitake or cremini in the fridge that need to get used, this is a great go-to. This pâté is every bit as rich and delicious as one made from meat, and even makes an indulgent paste for a beef Wellington. Soaking the walnuts overnight in red wine gives them more flavor and makes them softer and creamier. It's a popular centerpiece on fall and winter cheese and charcuterie boards garnished with some fresh thyme and pieces of walnut and served with Pine and Porcini Crackers (page 167). Once people know it's mushrooms—it looks mousy brown and somewhat suspect—they get excited to eat it.

_____

In a small bowl, soak the walnuts in red wine for at least 3 hours and up to 12.

In a medium pan over medium heat, melt the butter and sauté the shallots until they are translucent.

Add the mushrooms, garlic, thyme, salt, and pepper. Stir and continue cooking until everything is nicely browned.

In a blender, or using an immersion blender, puree the walnuts and mushroom mixture until smooth. The texture should be thick but spreadable.

Serve immediately, or refrigerate in a tightly covered container for a week.

Sautéed Mushrooms with Buckwheat Soba and Miso

MAKES 2 SERVINGS

2 tablespoons unsalted butter or olive oil

1 leek, cut into half-moons (about 1 cup)

1 garlic clove, minced

4 cups mushrooms, any type, sliced and diced

2 cups kale or other winter green, chopped into bite-size pieces

1 teaspoon kosher salt

7 to 9 ounces buckwheat soba noodles (see note)

2 teaspoons sesame oil

2 cups water

2 tablespoons yellow or red miso

1 teaspoon grated ginger

1 teaspoon sriracha (optional)

Seaweed Gomasio (page 83), for garnish

This is a very quick, easy weeknight dinner that feels deeply satisfying. My friend Sasha, who has been hunting mushrooms for thirty years, called me for advice on what to do with a cauliflower mushroom. So I suggested this Japanese cuisine–inspired dish, which is not in his Italian-centric mushroom recipe rotation. He and his partner enjoyed it so much, he wants to go take cooking classes in Kyoto. This is good with all mushrooms, and you can easily pad it with some store-bought shiitakes. If you use chanterelles or hedgehogs, dry-cook them to get the moisture out first. This recipe calls for pure buckwheat soba noodles because they have a firmer texture that feels more elegant to me. But I also love the ones made with flour, with a softer, more comfort-food feel to them, and they are much less expensive, so feel free to swap them out.

———————————————

Bring a large pot of water to a boil.

In a medium sauté pan, melt the butter and add the leeks; sauté for 2 to 3 minutes. Then add the garlic and mushrooms and sauté for a few minutes, and when the mushrooms are soft and leeks turning brown, add the kale. Continue to cook until everything is softened. Add the salt and turn off the heat.

To the boiling water, add the soba and cook according to package directions, or 4 to 8 minutes, while occasionally stirring. Taste halfway to see if they're done; they should be firm and a little al dente but not hard. Immediately drain and rinse with cold water. Put noodles back into the large pot and toss them in the sesame oil to prevent them from sticking. ⟶

Note: Buckwheat soba varies greatly in price—that's because some are made with only buckwheat flour with no salt or wheat flour. Buckwheat is a seed, not a wheat, so pure buckwheat noodles will cost more than buckwheat noodles that are also made with regular flour.

TO MAKE THE MISO SAUCE:

Boil the water and then remove from heat and let it cool slightly. In a small bowl, add miso to the water and whisk until smooth. Add the grated ginger, and sriracha if you like a little heat, and stir.

Add the mushroom mixture into the noodle pot. Toss until it's well mixed. Put into two bowls, and pour the miso sauce over each of them.

Garnish with gomasio and serve.

PORCINI

Boletus edulis

Porcini is Italian for "little piglets," and finding them gives me the biggest dopamine hit. I don't know what it is about the tawny, rounded cap, but my heart flutters. For these, you want a solid rainfall followed by sunlight. Then more rain, more sun. Count out twenty-one days following the first rain of the season. Or seven or fourteen, depending on whom you ask. Fungi can be incredibly unreliable, but that's also what makes them exciting. Coastal California porcini season starts around November and lasts a few months. The Sierras have spring and summer porcini (*Boletus rex-veris*), depending on the rain patterns. They occur in the spring, summer, and fall in the Pacific Northwest. Alaska has them throughout the spring, summer, and fall. Check and make sure it's legal to take them in a given area and what the limits are.

Fall porcini are often found under pines in California. They may also be under spruce, fir, and occasionally oak. Look for "shrumps," or "mushrumps," which are little mounds of pine needles. Porcini seem to like dappled light, so scan areas where tree limbs meet the sunlight of a meadow.

Indicator mushrooms will often grow near porcini. These can be the *Amanita muscaria*, red with white dots, or the white *Clitopilus prunulus*. When you discover porcini somewhere, they may come back in that same spot year after year, or they may not ever come back. Or someone will beat you to them next year. So enjoy the moment! When you find your good spot, treat it like a nude selfie and be very discriminate about whom you show it to.

If you find a "number two" porcini (see Stages of a Mushroom's Life, page 93), you might want to remove the spores before cooking them, as they could get mushy. The spores have a lot of flavor, so keep these for a soup broth, but if the spores are too big and blown out, toss them. If I find a lovely number two porcini, I might cut off the damaged parts and make Porcini Butter (page 106), and use the best sections for skewers. Avoid washing porcini with water. Just rub them with a dry, clean cloth. Store them in paper in the fridge in the crisper or a container lined with paper towels.

Grilled Porcini on Rosemary Skewers with Porcini Butter

MAKES 8 SKEWERS

2 small to medium young porcinis

½ cup extra-virgin olive oil

1 tablespoon sea salt

8 rosemary branches, leaves removed except for at the tip, and soaked in water for at least 2 to 3 hours

⅓ cup Porcini Butter (recipe follows)

Mushroom skewers are a life hack. They're simple, elegant, and people seem to like the novelty of eating food off a stick. You can grill these over a smoldering live fire with a grate or on a grill at home. I have a ton of rosemary bushes in the vicinity, so I use the rosemary branches as skewers, which impart a wonderful flavor to the porcini. I just soak them first in water so they don't light on fire. Only use number one or number two porcini, or the best parts that don't have any visible damage. Use some less-pristine parts of a porcini or older porcini to make the Porcini Butter served with them. These can be plated and served with warm sourdough bread and a side of the butter, or right off the stick while sitting around the fire.

Slice the porcini lengthwise, about a quarter of an inch thick. You'll have small pieces that you can't skewer, so set those aside to make the butter.

Brush with the oil and sprinkle with a little salt on both sides.

Gently thread them onto the skewers up to the part where the leaves remain. Be careful not to break the porcinis.

Heat a grill to 350 degrees F. Place them on the grill with the herb part of the skewer away from the flame.

Grill on each side for 5 to 7 minutes, or until browned.

Remove from the heat and set on a platter; add a teaspoon of the Porcini Butter on each one while they're still hot. Salt to taste.

1 cup unsalted butter, divided

1 shallot, minced

½ cup porcini, cut into small cubes or slices

1 clove garlic

½ teaspoon rosemary, minced

½ teaspoon salt

Pinch of freshly ground black pepper

PORCINI BUTTER

If you have some cosmetically challenged pieces of porcini, whip up this butter and gift to your favorite people, or serve at a dinner with the skewers, or freeze it for later. It's super rich—with the porcini flavor going beyond a compound butter.

———————————————————

In a bowl, let ½ cup of the butter warm to room temperature.

In a small saucepan over medium-low heat, melt the other ½ cup of the butter. Add the shallot, stir, and a minute later add the porcini and garlic.

Sauté and then add the rosemary, salt, and pepper.

When everything is soft and cooked through, add to the room temperature butter. With an immersion blender, puree into a smooth paste. (You can also make this with a blender, but it's a pain to clean afterward.)

Store in 4-ounce mason jars in the fridge. It will be good for 1 to 2 months, or freeze it for up to a year.

Campfire Porcini Risotto

MAKES 8 SERVINGS

- 10 cups Mushroom "Bone" Broth (page 96)
- ½ cup extra-virgin olive oil, divided
- 1 yellow onion, chopped
- 2 garlic cloves, minced
- 3 cups arborio or short-grain white rice
- 2 cups white wine
- 1 tablespoon mixed fresh herbs (such as thyme, sage, and rosemary), finely diced
- 1 teaspoon kosher salt
- ½ teaspoon freshly ground black pepper
- ½ pound porcini, diced
- 1 cup freshly grated aged sheep or cow cheese (such as pecorino Romano), plus more for garnish
- Porcini and Pine Tip Salt (page 168) or other finishing salt

This is my go-to dish for autumn mushroom camp that I prepare over a live fire after a mushroom forage. It's a perfect warming dish on a chilly fall day. The smoke from the campfire adds another layer of rich flavor. But keep in mind, you need constant stirring, as the heat won't necessarily be even under the skillet.

Arborio is a thick-grained rice that can absorb a lot of liquid and still keep its texture. Crisp the rice in oil first to help it retain structure while it absorbs the flavors in the broth, resulting in a soft, starchy, velvety dish. Stir it frequently so it cooks evenly and gives off its starch, but not so much that it turns sticky and mushy. The final product should be soft and silky. Keep a few beautiful porcini slices to sauté and garnish on top. I like to serve this with a baguette that has been warmed over the fire and a simple salad with a crunchy texture like the Seaweed and Citrus Salad (page 23).

Make a fire and let the wood burn down to a low flame, just before coals. Set a large cast-iron skillet over the fire with the handle pointing outward so it doesn't get too hot.

In the skillet, heat the oil and sauté the onions until soft. Then add the garlic. Stir for a few seconds.

Add the rice and stir until it's coated with the hot oil and gets toasty on the outside. You may need to add more oil.

Add the wine and cook until it has evaporated.

Add a few cups of broth and stir the rice until the broth is almost absorbed.

Keep stirring, and move your skillet every so often if one section is bubbling hot while the other is not cooking as quickly.

Add a few cups more of the broth and stir again. Add the salt and pepper.

Scatter the herbs and stir.

Add a few cups more of the broth and then the porcini.

When the rice has absorbed the liquid, add the remaining broth and the cheese.

Split into bowls and garnish with extra cheese and a sprinkle of the Porcini and Pine Tip Salt.

CHANTERELLES

Chanterelles grow from mycelium, or the underground web that creates a symbiotic relationship with tree roots. When it rains, the mycelia pump water into the fruit so they can spring up and spread their spores. Along with autumn rains, chanterelles seem to like a cold snap. Chanterelles can start as early as November in Northern California and continue throughout the winter and into the spring. In the Pacific Northwest, they can start in midsummer at higher elevations and continue until it frosts.

Chanterelles particularly seem to grow with oak trees, and they can pop up in a variety of places—along driveways and walking paths, the local ballpark. The golden chanterelle can be spotted poking through dirt and leaves. Its bright-yellow color is a giveaway. They are trumpet-shaped with wavy ridges. Their stems tend to be thick, and their flesh dense and off-white. They often have a mild, fruity apricot scent.

When you find one, be sure and look under the leaves nearby for more, as they tend to grow in a flush. Mark this spot somewhere, as they may come back to the same places every year.

Beware of Look-Alikes!

Some mushrooms look like chanterelles but are not. The "false chanterelle," or *Hygrophoropsis aurantiaca*, has disappointed me before. They are similar in color to the golden chanterelle, but their gills are different. Once you see them side by side, it's easy to tell the difference. As well, Jack O' Lantern (*Omphalotus olearius*) mushrooms grow out of wood, and you'll often see them at the base of trees with a golden color and flutelike shape. They can be growing from wood that's under dirt, so seem to be from mycelium but are not. A mushroom hunter once told me, "Trust your eyes—they know the truth. Your brain will trick you."

Both the false chanterelle and the Jack O' Lantern have straight, deep gills, while the golden chanterelle has shallow, forking ridges for gills.

Fire-Roasted Kabocha Squash with Chanterelles

MAKES 4 SERVINGS

2 small to medium kabo-
cha squashes

4 cups Mushroom
"Bone" Broth (page
96), divided

1 pound chanterelles,
washed and torn into
long strips (about 3
cups)

3 tablespoons unsalted
butter, divided

1 medium shallot, finely
diced

3 cups kale, deribbed
and cut into small
pieces

1 teaspoon kosher salt

Pinch of freshly ground
black pepper

Pinch of Urfa chili or red
chili flakes

½ cup shaved Romano
cheese

½ cup toasted walnuts,
roughly chopped

Finishing salt

The autumn flavors of squash and chanterelles just seem right together. I make this at camp by cooking the whole squash directly in the hot coals of a campfire and serving the roasted squash topped with the sautéed chanterelles on a long rustic board. It disappears fast. If you don't have the mushroom broth, just put a little butter or olive oil in the squash so it doesn't dry out. But if you do cook it with the broth, it can be reused later to make the Campfire Porcini Risotto (page 108). You want the squash to be sitting flat in the embers and not rolling around and splashing out its broth. This can be served alongside something autumnal like pork tenderloin or enjoyed as a main dish.

Cut the tops off the squashes and set aside. Remove the seeds and pierce the flesh inside all over with a fork.

Pour the mushroom broth inside each squash, put the top back on it, and set in the hot coals of a campfire. (Alternatively, cook in a 375-degree oven for 40 to 45 minutes.)

In a cast-iron skillet on the campfire, dry-cook the chanterelles to get the water out. Remove the mushrooms from the pan and set aside.

Add 2 tablespoons of the butter and sauté the shallot until soft and translucent. ⟶

Add the kale and the chanterelles to the shallots. Add a little more butter if need be. Sauté and sprinkle with the salt, pepper, and Urfa chili.

When the chanterelles are caramelized and the kale soft, set aside in pan but keep warm.

Use a fork to test each squash to see if it's done. It should easily pierce the flesh and skin. Remove from the embers and pour out the broth (or set aside to reuse). When they're cool enough to handle, put them on a platter and slice horizontally in half with a chef's knife into four pieces for each squash. Smash down so that it lies flat on a cutting board or plate.

Top each squash with the chanterelle mixture.

Sprinkle with the cheese, walnuts, and finishing salt and serve immediately.

Chanterelles with Cedar-Planked Black Cod

MAKES 4 SERVINGS

2 pounds black cod fillet, skin on

1 teaspoon kosher salt

1 pound of golden chanterelles, cleaned and shredded

¼ cup water

1 heaping tablespoon miso

1 tablespoon grated ginger

½ teaspoon red chili flakes

2 tablespoons unsalted butter

2 large shallots, cut into thin slivers

½ pound of shiitake mushrooms, sliced

1 teaspoon fresh thyme

½ teaspoon freshly ground black pepper

1 teaspoon Seaweed Gomasio (page 83), for garnish

Black cod is one of the most delicious fish to come out of the Pacific. It's oily and rich—and has twice the omega-3s as salmon, so it's super healthy. It's sustainably caught—usually with pots, which means there's little chance of bycatch. And it's plentiful and available almost year-round on the West Coast. Cooking black cod fillets on cedar planks gives them a mild smoky, woody flavor, and you don't have to scrape a grill clean afterward. You'll need a cedar plank untreated by any chemicals, soaked in water overnight, and large enough for black cod fillets. This way it won't catch fire on the grill, and the dampness will steam the fish and give it a delicate forest flavor. Since this is such an oily fish, it won't dry out if you leave it on a little long, but it can get mushy if cooked over low heat for longer periods of time. The aesthetic of the fish fillet on cedar plank covered with sautéed wild mushrooms in a miso sauce feels rustic and abundant.

Sprinkle the black cod with the kosher salt, and let sit 30 minutes to bring it up to room temperature.

Heat the grill to 400 degrees F.

In a large skillet, dry-cook the chanterelles until moisture stops sweating out. Remove from the pan and set aside.

In a small saucepan over medium heat, warm the water. Add the miso and whisk it until dissolved. Stir in the ginger and chili flakes. Remove from heat.

In another skillet over medium heat, add the butter and sauté the shallots until softened. Add the shiitakes and cook for about 3 to 4 minutes; then add the chanterelles back into the skillet. Sauté together.

Add the miso along with the thyme and pepper. Sauté together and then simmer on low.

Put the black cod on cedar planks and place on the grill, then close the cover.

Cook for 10 to 20 minutes, or until the flesh starts to separate at the top.

Remove from the grill.

Either serve on the plank or, using a spatula, remove from the wooden plank, keeping the fillet intact. Place it on a platter. Cover with the sautéed chanterelles and garnish with the gomasio.

Note: Black cod have a lot of tiny, soft bones in them. You can try and remove them with a tweezer before cooking, but you won't get them all. I just warn people that there are small, soft bones in them before serving.

OYSTER MUSHROOMS

Oyster mushrooms grow in stunning fractal patterns, their curled edges and lobes fanning the span of hardwood trees that are often dying or have fallen. These shelflike clusters often have mushrooms in various stages, from newly bloomed to old and fanned out. They are not damaging host trees, rather they are saprotrophs, like turkey tail or reishi mushrooms, that decompose ill or dead trees, putting energy back into the forest ecosystem. Interestingly, oyster mushrooms are carnivorous as they prey on nematodes, or tiny worms. The mushrooms use the nitrogen of their prey to help them with their rapid growth.

They are not only easily found in the wild but very simple to cultivate. Since they aren't mushrooms that grow on mycelium on tree roots, if you decide to grow mushrooms at home, these are your starter mushrooms. You can purchase blocks filled with mycelium, or create your own from items like rice and oyster shells. Or inoculate logs with their spores. They grow quickly, and there are a lot of varieties of them, from pink-pearly ones to blue to phoenix, queen, and king. Their robust growth and culinary versatility make them a global favorite. They usually don't need to be washed; just brush them off with a towel and trim any dirty stems. These mushrooms have been named after the beloved bivalve, as they smell bittersweet when raw; but when cooked, they have a savory seafood-like flavor and texture.

Oyster Mushrooms with Grilled Radicchio and Persimmons

MAKES 4 SERVINGS

¼ cup extra-virgin olive oil

2 tablespoons apple cider vinegar

2 teaspoons fish sauce (or vegan seaweed fish sauce)

2 cloves garlic, minced

2 teaspoons minced ginger

½ teaspoon kosher salt

¼ teaspoon freshly ground black pepper

1 head of radicchio di Treviso, cut into 1-inch pieces

1 medium Fuyu persimmon, firm but ripe, cut into ½-inch squares

5 to 10 oyster mushrooms, cleaned, trimmed, and broken into bite-size pieces

1 teaspoon Seaweed Gomasio (page 83), for garnish

This winter dish hits all the pleasure spots. The mushrooms are savory, the radicchio bitter, the persimmon sweet. Toss them in the umami marinade and then grill for a savory, warm "salad." This is a delicious stand-alone dish or can be served alongside just about any protein—from steak to rockfish to pork tenderloin to tempeh. I love this alongside crispy sand dabs.

In a small bowl, whisk together the oil, vinegar, fish sauce, garlic, ginger, salt, and pepper and set aside.

Add the radicchio, persimmons, and mushrooms to three separate mixing bowls. Divide the marinade among the bowls and toss to coat.

In a cast-iron or heavy-bottomed skillet over medium heat, add the persimmons and cook for a few minutes, or until they turn a deeper shade of orange.

Add the mushrooms and cook 3 to 6 minutes until they start turning golden brown. Add the radicchio and simmer to soften, but don't cook the moisture completely out of it.

Divide into bowls, and garnish with the gomasio.

Smoked and Pickled Oyster Mushrooms

MAKES ONE 16-OUNCE JAR

1 cup apple cider vinegar

1 cup water

1 tablespoon sugar

1 tablespoon plus ¼ teaspoon kosher salt, divided

2 cups wood chips (such as cherry, apple, or hickory; see note)

3 cups small, firm oyster mushrooms, brushed and trimmed

½ cup sesame oil

¼ teaspoon freshly ground black pepper

⅛ teaspoon red chili flakes

1 clove garlic

1 tablespoon freshly grated ginger

The only problem with these smoky pickled mushrooms is that you don't know if the people in your life really love you for who you are, or if they are only interested in your mushroom pickles. These are a big, big hit on a cheese platter: soft and tangy, with just a hint of smoke. Just put out a little bowl of toothpicks next to them and watch them disappear. In the fall when oysters are blooming, I'll serve them alongside homemade crackers with russet apple slices and aged cheddar cheese, sprinkled with the Porcini and Pine Tip Salt (page 168). This is also delicious with little shiitake mushrooms. But use small mushrooms—don't slice up big ones as they'll be too soft and floppy.

In a small saucepan over low heat, combine the vinegar, water, sugar, and a tablespoon of the salt. Stir until the sugar and salt dissolve. Remove from the heat and set aside to cool.

In a medium bowl, soak the wood chips in water for 30 minutes.

Preheat the oven to 350 degrees F.

After the chips are soaked through, cover the bottom of a deep roasting pan with aluminum foil and spread the chips over the foil.

Place a grate over the wood chips and set the pan aside.

In a medium bowl, toss the mushrooms with the sesame oil, ¼ teaspoon of the salt, pepper, and chili flakes.

Spread out on the baking grate. Then cover them tightly with foil.

Cook in the oven for 15 minutes, or until soft but not soggy. ⟶

In a clean 16–ounce jar with a lid, pour in the vinegar mixture, leaving about ¼ inch of headspace.

Add the garlic and ginger and put the lid on. Refrigerate for 2 days, then enjoy.

They'll keep in the fridge up to 2 weeks. Or water-bath can them for long-term storage.

VARIATION: USE A SMOKER

Note: Using hickory wood chips results in a stronger smoke flavor, whereas cherrywood results in a more delicate flavor. I like to use cherry.

If you have a small smoker, such as a donabe, this recipe is even easier. I use my donabe for about everything—it's portable and has a lovely elegance to it. So if you happen to have one, here's a recipe for that. Add the wood chips on a medium flame for 5 to 10 minutes. Wait until the wood is on fire and smoking. Layer your mushrooms tossed in oil and spices on the screen. Keep them in a single row, not stacked. When the wood is smoking, cover the lid, seal with water, and turn off the flame to cook for 5 to 10 minutes, until all are soft.

BLACK TRUMPETS

Craterellus cornucopioides

They're called horns of plenty, black chanterelles, and in French, *trompettes de la mort*, trumpets of death. To me, they taste like delicious dirt, a savory distillation of the forest ground and air. They appear in pine and Douglas fir forests later in the season, often after fall porcini season has ended.

They grow low to the ground, camouflaged among dark leaves, and in the shadows of fallen logs. It helps to not focus your eyes, but rather scan the ground from the corners of your eyes, looking for pattern disruption and negative space—sometimes a black patch on the forest floor, upon closer look, means black trumpets. Once you spot a couple, it gets easier. Some people think if you "pick clean," you don't need to wash them, but grit and pine needles get easily caught in their upturned horns. So to clean, use your thumb to open them and rub out any detritus, and then run them under water in a colander to rinse off any remaining grit.

These don't have a lot of water in them like chanterelles, and so don't need to be dry-cooked. If you love black trumpets as much as I do, be sure to check out the Stinging Nettle Gnocchi with Brown-Butter Black Trumpets on page 207 in the Wild Greens section as well.

Campfire Black Trumpet Flatbread with Pine Tips and Feta

MAKES 4
FLATBREADS

⅓ cup pine nuts

½ cup unsalted butter

1 yellow onion, sliced

2 to 3 cups black trumpets, cleaned, larger ones shredded into bite-size pieces

Pinch of kosher salt

1 pound pizza dough, divided into quarters (store-bought is fine)

Extra-virgin olive oil, for brushing

1 tablespoon za'atar, divided

1 cup (about 6 ounces) crumbled feta cheese, divided

4 pine tips (about 4 tablespoons), cleaned and finely chopped, divided

Flatbreads are really just pizza with a creative license. You can put about anything on them, and they don't have to be round. When making this flatbread on a campfire, I like to add some dry, open pine cones to the fire for a little extra pine flavor in the smoke. Avoid the young green pine cones with lots of resin still on them as they will smoke and impart a glue-like essence. Pine and fir tips are the young pale-green growth that appears each spring. These have a lemony flavor to them with a slight piney essence—as the needles get older, the pine flavor gets stronger. This recipe is for campfire flatbreads, but you can easily make these indoors with a really hot oven. They're best served while warm with a simple salad on the side.

Let the pizza dough rise for at least 30 minutes before using

Build your fire to a medium to low flame with red coals.

In a cast-iron pan on the grill over the fire, add the pine nuts and toast them until they are light brown. Set them aside.

Add the butter and melt, then the onions. Stir a few times and when they turn translucent, add the mushrooms. Sprinkle the salt over them and stir, cooking until the black trumpets are limp and a much darker shade of brown, 4 to 5 minutes.

Remove from the fire and set aside. ⟶

Use a roller or toss the dough with your hands. Doing both is ideal, but you're camping and don't want to pack a bulky roller, so just hand-toss or use a clean water or wine bottle to roll it out. Start in the center, and roll in each direction, like it's pie dough. If using your hands, pick it up with both hands, pinching with thumb and forefingers, like you're about to hang a piece of laundry to dry. Then rotate it so the weight thins itself out. You can also make a fist and hang it over your knuckles, rotating until it thins out.

Line a cast-iron pan with parchment paper.

Brush oil on the dough and place it on the parchment-paper-lined pan. Put it in the fire for 4 to 5 minutes. (By prebaking on one side, the crust will be a little crispier under the toppings.)

Flip the crust and sprinkle the za'atar spice over the exposed side.

Layer one quarter of the onions and black trumpets on each flatbread, and then sprinkle the feta over them. Finish with the pine nuts and pine tips. Put this back onto the fire.

Let cook for about 7 minutes, or until the sides are brown and bubbly.

HEDGEHOGS

Hydnum repandum

Hedgehogs don't have the same sexy rep of porcini or chanterelle, perhaps because they are named after adorable rodents, but they are every bit as delicious. They're also cute and easy to spot, due to their chubby amber and beige-hued caps that contrast with the moss- and pine-covered forest floor. And hedgehogs are considered a good mushroom for beginners to learn, as their cap underside is unique—rather than gills or spores, there are tiny quills, like those found on the hedgehog. When fresh, they're highly versatile and can be prepared like chanterelles. I recommend dry-cooking these also, as they have a lot of water. Just caramelize them in butter with leeks or shallots. Their flavor is a little more nutty, meaty than the chanterelle.

They grow in mixed coniferous forests. I've mostly found them under pine trees and tan oak from December into March when the rains are steady. They are often small and will grow together in small clusters. When picking these mushrooms, cut them off at the base and give them a quick brush with your porcini knife or a paper towel. Once home, they can be rinsed, but that doesn't really do much, as fallen needles become embedded in them, and they can be laborious to clean—like pulling out splinters. If the mushrooms have grown together, pull them apart and then remove any grit or pine needles. Or you can just have some pine needles in your mushroom—it won't hurt anyone.

Hedgehog Mushroom Dumpling Soup with Chrysanthemum Greens

MAKES 4 SERVINGS

5 cups Mushroom "Bone" Broth (page 96)

1 cup small hedgehog mushrooms, sliced

16 Hedgehog Mushroom Dumplings (recipe follows)

2 cups chrysanthemum greens, washed and roughly chopped

4 tablespoons sriracha or gochujang sauce (optional)

2 tablespoons sesame oil

Seaweed Gomasio (page 83), for garnish

In the fall you most likely can urban-forage chrysanthemum greens; just make sure you're not vandalizing someone's garden. If you grow these flowers, you can just loot your own yard. These greens are often available for purchase at Asian grocery stores or from farmers' market vendors who specialize in Asian produce. They are known as a spring and fall green, but I find them in California in midwinter, about when hedgehogs start appearing (but if you can't find any, use any leafy greens like kale, chard, or collards). The greens are wonderful both cooked and raw, with a flavor that's grassy and a bit floral, leaving a slightly bitter taste. They tend to get mushy if over-cooked, so add them at the very end.

In a medium saucepan over medium-high heat, warm the broth. When bubbles appear on the bottom, add the mushrooms. Put the lid on the pot and let cook for about 5 minutes.

Add the dumplings. Cook for 2 to 3 minutes if fresh, or 4 to 6 minutes if frozen, moving them in the hot broth gently so they don't break apart. When they are translucent and floating, they should be done. (If using frozen dumplings, I make an extra dumpling and test it to make sure it's not still cold in the center. But if they cook too long, they fall apart.)

When the dumplings are cooked through, remove them from the broth and add the wild greens. Let these soften in the broth.

Divide into four bowls and to each, add a tablespoon of sriracha or gochujang sauce, a swirl of sesame oil, and a garnish of gomasio.

HEDGEHOG MUSHROOM DUMPLINGS

2 pounds (about 2 cups)
diced hedgehog
mushrooms

¼ cup extra-virgin olive
oil or unsalted butter

1 medium shallot,
minced

1 clove of garlic, minced

1 tablespoon fresh gin-
ger, peeled and finely
grated

¼ head of Napa cab-
bage, finely shredded
(about 2 cups)

1½ tablespoons tamari

1 tablespoon sesame oil

1 teaspoon kosher salt

1 teaspoon ground
green Szechuan pep-
percorns (optional)

½ teaspoon red chili
flakes

24 dumpling wrappers

1 egg

Hedgehogs, like chanterelles, don't freeze well—they lose their shape and luster and get discolored and limp. So if I find myself with extras, I'll make duxelles out of them and then freeze them. Since the mushrooms have been dry-cooked and then sautéed in butter or oil, they hold up to freezing. Later, they can be used for beef Wellington or used as toppings for crostini or a mushroom pâté for a cheese board. One of my favorite ways to store them is to put them into dumplings. These dumplings are great to pull out of your freezer to feed last-minute visitors.

In a frying pan over medium-low heat, dry-cook the mushrooms until the water cooks out of them. Remove the mushrooms from the frying pan.

Add the oil and sauté the shallots for a few minutes until translucent.

Add the garlic, ginger, and cabbage; stir-fry until browned, 5 to 8 minutes.

Add the mushrooms back in, along with the tamari, sesame oil, salt, pepper, and chili. Continue cooking on low heat until any moisture is gone, the cabbage is thoroughly cooked, and the filling has a thick, sticky consistency. Remove from the heat.

Line the dumpling wrappers on a baking sheet.

Break the egg into a small bowl, add a tablespoon of water, and lightly beat with a fork.

Scoop a tablespoon of mushroom mixture into the center of the wrapper. Using a finger or brush, run the egg wash over half the dumpling wrapper at the edge. Press the other half over, sealing the sides of the dumpling with your fingers.

When you've used all your filling, lay the dumplings flat on a baking sheet lined with parchment paper and place them in the freezer. Transfer to a ziplock bag once frozen.

MORELS

Morchella

Morels are a delicious fungus with caps of velvety dark ribs and beige pitted surfaces; they are prized for their rich, savory flavor. While some types of morels grow naturally in mixed-conifer forests, when there are forest fires, huge flushes of them can occur the following year, and even after two or three years in the burned area. Foraging for these is a great way to learn about forest fire and regeneration.

When out hunting morels in the late spring / early summer, look for burn areas, but also pay attention to altitude. You need rain for them to flush. They start appearing at lower altitudes, around three thousand feet, and start blooming up the mountain as the snow melts. However, if a fire rages too hot, it burns everything, including the mycelium. These areas look apocalyptic. Yet in the zones not decimated but where the burn moved through, some of the trees are left untouched. It was almost as if the fire moved like a river delta through the thicket, burning some trees and just singeing others, while other trees were left completely alone. Signs of new growth spring up quickly. You'll see tiny forests of tiny pines poking up through charred dirt. Be careful of the burned root pits, as these are deep holes. But morels may be growing there too.

Nobody really knows why morels follow fire. Some scientists speculate it could have something to do with changes in the soil or the lack of competition from other organisms after a fire, while others believe the shifting availability of food and nutrients is responsible.

Since mushrooms are regenerative by nature, they in turn help the forest grow back after a fire. It might be by breaking down nutrients in the soil or spreading nutrients throughout the burned ground via animals that eat them.

For over thirteen thousand years, Indigenous people in California used controlled burns to manage the lands they hunted, fished, and foraged. They viewed this as tending the lands. And in return they got delicious morels.

Morels, Asparagus, Fava Beans, and Fiddlehead Ferns with Burrata

MAKES 4 TO 8 APPETIZER SERVINGS

2 tablespoons unsalted butter or olive oil

1 cup fresh morels (about ½ pound), sliced in half, or quarters if large (see note)

1 cup asparagus, cut into ¼-inch pieces

½ cup fresh fava beans

6 to 8 fiddlehead ferns (boiled for 12 minutes)

1 teaspoon kosher salt

½ teaspoon freshly ground black pepper

Pinch of Urfa or other smoky chili powder (optional)

1 large piece of burrata (or two smaller ones)

2 tablespoons peppery, young extra-virgin olive oil (such as Olio Nuovo)

2 tablespoons fresh lemon juice

1 teaspoon finishing salt

Fresh parsley for garnish (optional)

Crusty baguette

This dish is pure springtime—it's fire and regeneration in one dish. Savory and bright green and creamy with a bit of acid and a reminder that the world is a wonderful place and springtime is more than a state of mind—it's a sensory delight promising good things to come. There are many variations for this, as long as you don't serve morels raw. If you use dried morels, soak them in hot water until they soften first and then cook them.

In a large saucepan over medium-high heat, melt the butter. Add the morels and sauté until soft.

Add the asparagus, fava beans, and fiddlehead ferns. Sauté for just a minute or two, until the greens become bright green. Sprinkle on the salt, pepper, and chili. Remove from the heat before they start to overcook.

Lay the burrata in the center of a platter, and arrange the morels and green vegetables around the burrata.

Drizzle the oil over the cheese and vegetables, then add the lemon juice.

Sprinkle the finishing salt and parsley over the burrata, and enjoy with a sliced baguette.

Note: If using dried morels, use about 1 ounce, and then reconstitute them in hot water.

Wild King Salmon Bellies with Roasted Morels and Peaches

MAKES 2 SERVINGS

4 to 6 king salmon bellies (9 to 12 ounces)

1 teaspoon kosher salt

½ cup extra-virgin olive oil, plus more for brushing

6 to 10 large morels (see note)

1 peach, halved, pit removed

2 teaspoons Porcini and Pine Tip Salt (page 168) or regular finishing salt

1 teaspoon fresh thyme

½ teaspoon finishing salt

Note: You want large morels so they don't fall through the grill grate. If you only have small morels, skewer them or cook in a pan.

My favorite parts of king salmon are the bellies. This is the fattiest and most flavorful part of the fish, along with the collar. And it's also much cheaper than fillets. At my local farmers' market, bellies and collars cost ten dollars a pound, while the fillets are up in the mid-twenty-dollar range. When grilled or roasted, these get crisp exteriors, but the rich fats make the centers super juicy. A live fire makes for some rock-star campfire cooking: sink into grilled morels and juicy peaches eaten with your fingers in the glow of a campfire, alternating sweet and savory bites.

Sprinkle the salmon bellies with the kosher salt and let them come up to room temperature.

Build your fire hot and then let it burn down to coals. Brush the salmon bellies with some oil so they don't stick to the grill. Put them on the grill and cook for 3 to 4 minutes on each side. Remove from the grill and let them sit for another 3 to 4 minutes.

Meanwhile, in a large bowl, toss the morels and peach halves in the oil, the Porcini and Pine Tip Salt, and fresh thyme.

Put the peach halves on the grill face down, then the morels. Cook both about 4 minutes on each side. The morels should be soft and pliable, and the peach halves a little caramelized; they will appear darker in color and softer in texture.

Remove the peaches and morels from the fire. Slice each half of the peach into four pieces.

Plate the salmon bellies and layer the morels and peach slices on top of them with some finishing salt.

OREGON BLACK AND OREGON SPRING WHITE TRUFFLES

Leucangium carthusianum, Tuber gibbosum

The first time I smelled a truffle, it reached inside me and made me want it more than anything in the world. I inhaled notes of violets and strawberries, toasted walnuts and aged cheese, earth after a rain, the intimate smell of someone I once loved. The aroma traveled through my body, lighting up pleasure centers that I hadn't known existed inside me. So during COVID lockdown, when I adopted a puppy, it was one with truffle hunting in its DNA. That is how I came to get my Lagotto Romagnolo, Florence Jayne Tartufa—a.k.a. Flora Jayne.

My dirty, happy, always hungry, willful little familiar moves through the world with her heart-shaped pink nose to the ground. We started training with an online course through the Truffle Dog Company out of Seattle, Washington. We practiced truffle nose training nightly—I infused Q-tips with truffle oil, stuffed them into metal tea balls, and hid these "marks" around the house. When she found them, I cheered and gave her (and the cats) treats. Early on, my cat Spike beat her to the marks, and I wondered if I might leash train him for walks in the woods for truffles.

Flora Jayne has shown a talent for truffle hunting Oregon white and Oregon black truffles in the Douglas fir forests of Washington, Oregon, and in Northern California. Everything we do together is a form of training, of developing wordless communication, of learning to move through the woods together. (I once asked her to find me the kombu in a big wet patch of seaweed and she led me to it. May have been a fluke, but she's pretty amazing.)

The truffle is the node that moves energy through the forest. And when I lift the dirty nugget to my nose and inhale deeply, I feel like I am experiencing the very essence of a wooded wonderland. I've asked the mushroom vendors at the local farmers' market if they sell Oregon black truffles, and they say "not very often" as the local chefs don't think these truffles smell like the ones they're used to serving. I've heard people growing European varieties of truffles in California wine country trash-talking our native truffles. Ironic, considering the same was said about their wines forty years ago.

Cheesy Truffle-Infused Pasta with Shaved Black Truffles

MAKES 4 SERVINGS

2 cups white flour

2 cups semolina flour

1 teaspoon kosher salt

4 large truffle-infused eggs, lightly beaten (page 138)

5 tablespoons truffle-infused butter (page 138)

1½ cups grated truffle-infused pecorino cheese (page 138), divided

1 ounce fresh truffle(s): 1 to 2 Oregon black truffles, or 3 to 4 small Oregon white truffles, brushed to remove dirt

1 teaspoon finishing salt

You can make this recipe with either the Oregon spring white or black truffle. (I have yet to find an Oregon winter truffle.) The Oregon spring white truffle has a classic truffle scent—garlicky and cheesy. These tend to be much smaller than the Oregon black truffles, but in the Pacific Northwest they are often found in the same areas. Oregon black truffles have a fruity, jammy scent, so they are great in fat-based desserts like ice cream and crème brûlée. But they are still delicious with savory foods. If you don't have a truffle pooch, native truffles are becoming more common at markets on the West Coast, and they make a big splash flavor-wise for the cost. This recipe uses three different types of truffle infusions in the dish and is topped with shaved raw truffle for maximum earthly delight.

_____

To make the pasta, in a large bowl, mix the flours and salt. Make a well in the center. Add the eggs to the center of the well and mix by hand, or use a stand mixer.

Scatter some flour onto your workspace and begin flattening and then folding the dough. Start to knead the dough, working out any air pockets. Then divide the dough into four equal parts. Wrap the parts in plastic wrap and let rest in the fridge for half an hour.

Remove the dough from the fridge, and keep the sections you aren't using covered with a cloth so they don't dry out.

Put one of the quarters through a pasta machine on the thickest setting. When it's flatter, almost sheetlike, fold it into thirds, and repeat two more times.

Put the rolled dough through the pasta machine on a noodle setting, such as fettuccine. Then gently lay the pasta onto a tray sprinkled with flour—semolina is best, but any kind will work. If the pasta feels sticky, you can hang it on a pasta rack or open a cupboard and hang it over the door.

To cook the pasta, bring a large pot of lightly salted water to a boil. Add the pasta and cook for 4 to 5 minutes, or until al dente.

Save ¼ cup of the pasta water.

Drain the pasta and return to the pot.

While the pasta is hot, add the truffle-infused butter, ¾ cup of the truffle-infused cheese, and the pasta water and gently mix until the noodles are coated.

Top with the remaining cheese and shave the truffle(s) over the pasta using a truffle shaver or a mandoline set on the thinnest-possible setting right before serving.

Finish with a generous sprinkle of finishing salt.

MAKING TRUFFLE INFUSIONS

Anything with fat can be infused by the volatile compounds of the truffle, which is good because Oregon truffles have a much shorter shelf life than European varieties and need to be used right away. I've never had luck making truffle salt—it dries them up and the salt doesn't have a carrier oil to hold the flavor. Same for dry rice—no luck. You can also preserve them by putting the odds and ends into honey, butter, or oil. But be warned, 99.9 percent of commercially sold truffle oil is pure skulduggery. It's a chemical compound that imitates the truffle in an exaggerated, steroided-out way. The real thing is much more subtle and sublime.

BUTTER: Wrap one large or two small truffles in a paper towel and put them into a glass container with a half stick of butter.

CHEESE: Put some in a glass container with 2 cups of pecorino cheese or one wedge.

CREAM: Either shave your truffle into 2 cups of cream, or put the truffle into a tea ball and hang it in a jar dangling over the cream. This can be used for the Black Truffle Crème Brûlée on page 141.

EGGS: The heady aroma of truffle is so strong that it will infuse eggs through their shells, so when I have a stash, the first thing I do is add them to a jar of whole, uncooked eggs. You can also wrap them in a paper towel so they don't absorb moisture and get soft. (It takes only one truffle to infuse many eggs, but add as many as you can fit in your infusions.) Leave the eggs in the jar overnight to infuse. Keep in mind, the more truffles you use and the longer they are with the eggs, the stronger the truffle flavor will be. But you want to use them before their magic fades, so use them as soon as possible.

Oregon White Truffles on Bone Marrow

MAKES 4 APPETIZER SERVINGS

4 small beef marrow bones, cut lengthwise

1 tablespoon grated Parmesan cheese (infused with truffles if possible, see page 138)

1 cup coarse salt

1 to 2 small Oregon white truffles

Finishing salt

Baguette

The Oregon white, *Tuber gibbosum*, is my Moby-Dick of truffles. They are small and pungent, and the scent may remind you of toasted hazelnuts, cheese, butter, and mild garlic along with lost love, tango music, and the earth after a rain. These were a favorite of Harvey Harkness, the California "Father of Mycology" in the late 1800s, where he found them near my home just north of the Golden Gate Bridge. A team of mycologists found them in my county and when the creator of *Peanuts*, Charles Schulz, who lived in nearby Sonoma County, got wind of this, he made Snoopy's alter ego "the World Famous Truffle Hound." Despite this, Flora Jayne and I have been surveying the area with no luck. She's found these in the Pacific Northwest and in far Northern California, so I know she'll find some local ones eventually under the right conditions.

Since white truffles are often very small, I don't build a meal around them, but rather an appetizer. This is one of my favorites.

Set the broiler to 500 degrees F.

On a baking sheet, place the bones marrow side up and roast for 10 minutes. When the marrow is soft and jiggly but the top of the bone crisp and brown, sprinkle on the cheese. Return to the broiler for about 2 minutes longer, until the cheese is melted and becomes crispy.

Remove from the oven.

Pour a small mound of coarse salt on each plate and set the bone in the center so it doesn't tip to the side.

Shave the Oregon white truffles on top of each marrow, and finish with a sprinkle of finishing salt.

Serve with a piece of warm, crusty bread.

Black Truffle Crème Brûlée with Preserved Sakura Cherry Blossoms

MAKES 6 SERVINGS

2 cups heavy cream

1 large Oregon black truffle

½ pod vanilla bean, or ½ teaspoon vanilla extract

5 egg yolks

4 tablespoons sugar

¼ teaspoon kosher salt

3 Preserved Sakura Cherry Blossoms (page 264), finely chopped

Native black truffles are earthy, jammy, and just wonderful. Since they have a dark fruit scent and infuse cream so well, they are wonderful in ice cream and other fat-based desserts. In this simple crème brûlée their flavor shines. You can save a bit of the truffle to shave on top, along with the salty, floral flavor of salt and ume-preserved cherry blossoms.

In a large bowl, add the heavy cream. Using a zester, grate three-quarters of the truffle into the cream. Slice the vanilla pod lengthwise, scraping the seeds into the cream. Then add the entire pod to the cream. Cover the bowl and refrigerate overnight.

The next day, preheat the oven to 325 degrees F.

In another bowl, whisk the egg yolks and sugar.

Strain the truffles and vanilla pod out of the cold cream.

Put the cream into a heavy-bottomed saucepan and heat on low, stirring constantly so it doesn't burn on the bottom.

Once it's simmering, pour about 1 cup of the mixture into the egg and sugar bowl, and whisk. (This is known as tempering, and this way the eggs won't cook when you put them in the hot cream.) Once these are blended, pour this mixture into the saucepan. Continue whisking for about 5 more minutes, or until there's an even consistency.

Place 4 to 6 ramekins in a large baking dish and pour in boiling water around the ramekins so it comes halfway up the sides. ⟶

Divide the custard mixture among the ramekins.

Bake about 45 minutes or until the edges of the custards are set but the centers still jiggle slightly.

Remove the ramekins from the water bath and let the custards cool. Chill in the refrigerator until firm, at least 2 hours.

This can be made up to 5 days in advance.

Before serving, sprinkle a thin layer of sugar over each one and use a torch or broiler flame to "burn" the sugar for a few minutes. It's also great just as it is.

Shave the remaining ¼ of the truffle and sprinkle the sakura cherry blossoms over the top.

MAKES ⅓ CUP

1 tablespoon truffle bits and pieces, shaved or cut as finely as possible

⅓ cup honey

TRUFFLE HONEY

Inevitably, when you shave a truffle, you have little bits left at the end that you don't want to shave because you might remove the tip of your finger getting it that close to the blade. I'll often use these bits for nose training with Flora Jayne, or preserve them in this honey, elevated with its extra-earthy flavor.

In a small jar, blend all the ingredients well.

Cover with a lid and store in a cupboard—no need to refrigerate.

CANDY CAP MUSHROOMS

Lactarius rubidus,
Lactarius rufulus

These small cinnamon-brown mushrooms don't give the dopamine hit in the field that finding the bigger fungi delicacies do. But once your eyes get trained, they're easy to identify, often plentiful, and their wow factor is in the finished product. Despite their brown hue, they tend to be easy to spot in the woods. The way to tell them apart from the hundreds of other little brown mushrooms (LBMs) is how their hollow stems snap with the little droplets of "milk" inside and on the underside of their caps. They are in the *Lactarius* genus—Latin for "milk producing," so these milk droplets are telltale. (Note, there are also larger, paler *Lactarius* that are NOT edible, so always consult with an expert when starting out.) But one forage with an expert and you should have it—particularly when you hold up the undersides to other LBMs.

If possible, I first slow-dry them in the sun all day. If you have a dehydrator, use it to finish drying them. If not, I then put them in the oven at the lowest-possible temperature for about ninety minutes—this is to avoid any mildew or rot from developing while they slowly dry. In the winter, it can be hard to find a dry, sunny day. I then lay them out on a plate or tray and let them finish drying completely. In the process of drying them indoors, they fill your house with a heady aroma of maple syrup. It's truly wonderful. And they taste like maple syrup too.

They can be cooked as savory mushrooms, but every so often you get a very bitter one, so I almost exclusively dry them and use them in desserts by infusing butter or cream with them. People are amazed that the delightful, strong maple flavor is coming from a mushroom. Anything that calls for cream—like custard, ice cream, crème brûlée, or whipped cream—will hold their flavor. You can infuse butter with them for delicious butter cookies. The dough can be made in advance and frozen.

Once dried, you can store candy caps in a glass jar with a tight lid for years.

Wild Trifle with Candy Cap Whipped Cream

MAKES 12 SERVINGS

2 large tangerines with thick skins (like Minneola tangelo)

6 medium eggs (pasture-raised if possible)

1 cup sugar, or ⅓ cup dried monk fruit sweetener

2½ cups ground hazelnuts or hazelnut flour

1 teaspoon baking powder

Butter or spray oil for pan

2 cups Candy Cap Whipped Cream (recipe follows)

½ cup berries (such as huckleberries, blueberries, or blackberries), optional

A trifle is what you make when you mess up a cake. If it sticks to the pan or crumbles or one side falls—make a trifle by cutting it into pieces and layering on whipped cream and fruit or nuts. Everyone loves it even more than they would that perfect cake that didn't happen. I love making trifles with a hybridized version of orange almond cake, a Middle Eastern recipe that is naturally gluten-free as it is made with almond flour instead of wheat flour. One day, I wanted to make orange almond cake but didn't have oranges or almond flour, so I improvised with Minneola tangelos and hazelnuts, and halved the sugar called for in the original recipe. I prefer the natural tart, sweet citrus flavor. Since this trifle is dense, moist, citrusy, and not too sweet, the candy cap–infused whipped cream is fabulous on top. When I'm making this for a more formal dinner party, I serve them in individual ramekins garnished with a sprig of mint.

Wash the tangerines and then boil them whole for 1 to 2 hours. They should be very soft.

Preheat the oven to 375 degrees F.

Remove the tangerines from the water and cut them in quarters, removing the pith from the center and any seeds. Using a food processor or immersion blender, puree them. You should have about 2 cups of puree.

In a large bowl, beat the eggs and sugar. Mix in the hazelnuts and baking powder, then add the puree. ⟶

Butter or oil a 9-inch springform pan, then add the batter.

Bake for an hour. Use a toothpick to test if the cake is done by inserting it into the center. If the batter sticks, bake a little longer.

When done, remove from the oven and let cool.

Assemble by cutting the cake into pieces and plating. Top each piece of cake with a scoop of Candy Cap Whipped Cream and sprinkle the berries over the whipped cream.

CANDY CAP WHIPPED CREAM

MAKES ABOUT
2½ CUPS

3 cups heavy cream

½ cup dried candy cap
  mushrooms

1 teaspoon sugar

This recipe is for your feral friends who will inevitably ask, "Really, this whipped cream is flavored with mushrooms?" It has a maple flavor with an earthy element.

———————————————

Infuse the cream overnight with the candy caps in a lidded container in the fridge.

The next day, strain out the candy caps. Using a whisk or electric mixer, beat the cream and sugar until the mixture is fluffy and light.

Candy Cap Old-Fashioned

MAKES 1 DRINK

2 ounces Candy Cap–
Infused Bourbon
(recipe follows)

3 dashes "Lost in the
Woods" Bitters (page
171) or Angostura
bitters

1 teaspoon water

Ice

1 orange slice

2 Luxardo maraschino
cherries

In a mixing glass, add the bourbon, bitters, and water.

Fill the glass with ice and stir until well chilled.

In the bottom of a highball glass, add the orange slice and cherries. You
can give these a quick muddle. Add a large ice cube.

Strain the bourbon mixture into the highball glass, and serve!

*MAKES ONE 750
ML BOTTLE*

1 (750 mL) bottle bour-
bon or rye whiskey

2 ounces dried candy
cap mushrooms

CANDY CAP-INFUSED BOURBON

The flavor of candy cap mushrooms will grow stronger the longer
they infuse the bourbon, but it might also get more bitter and funky.
So taste on occasion to find your sweet spot. You can use these
mushrooms in any bourbon-forward cocktail.

_____

In a quart-size mason jar, add both ingredients and shake.

Cover the jar with a lid and put in a cupboard overnight, or up to
a month.

Candy Cap Mushroom Shortbread Cookies

MAKES 30 COOKIES

2 tablespoons dried rose petals (can substitute dried peonies)

½ cup plus 1 teaspoon sugar, divided

1 cup (8 ounces) salted European-style butter (such as Kerrygold), room temperature

3 tablespoons finely ground dried candy cap mushrooms (from ¼ cup loosely packed dried whole mushrooms)

2 cups all-purpose flour, plus more for dusting

Marla Aufmuth, the photographer for this book, perfected the candy cap cookie. And she's obsessed with them. She says, "The smell of maple permeates the kitchen, and it still blows my mind that it's actually the smell of candy cap mushrooms. This crisp-crunchy cookie is a showstopper, especially once you tell people what's in it." This recipe calls for cutout cookies, but you can also shape all the dough into a log about 2½ inches in diameter, refrigerate for at least an hour tightly wrapped in plastic wrap, then slice into ½-inch-thick rounds for slice-and-bake cookies.

Grind the rose petals and 1 teaspoon of the sugar in a spice grinder or with a mortar and pestle.

In a large mixing bowl with a hand mixer, beat together the butter and ½ cup of the sugar on medium-high speed until pale and fluffy.

In a separate bowl, thoroughly mix the candy cap mushrooms with the flour. Add to the butter-sugar mixture on low speed until it forms a stiff dough. If the dough is being stubborn, use your hands to form a ball.

Divide the dough into two rounds about ¾ inch thick, cover each tightly with plastic wrap, and chill for at least an hour.

Preheat the oven to 350 degrees F.

Line two baking sheets with parchment paper. ⟶

Remove one round of dough from the fridge at a time. Generously dust your work surface and rolling pin with flour and roll out the dough ¼ inch thick. If the dough feels too hard to roll, let it sit for a few minutes, until the butter softens.

Cut out the cookies using a cookie cutter.

Place the cookies on the prepared baking sheets about an inch apart.

Bake for 15 to 20 minutes, or until the cookies are a light-golden color and the cookies are cooked through.

Immediately add rose petal–sugar mix and lightly press into the center so they stick.

They will get crisper as they cool.

Trees and the Understory

Some species of tree are more promiscuous than others and can enter into relationships with many different fungal species.

—MERLIN SHELDRAKE, *ENTANGLED LIVES*

~~~~~~~~~~~~~~~~~~~~

THE PINE TREE SEEMS TO BE one of the more fungi-promiscuous of trees. Beneath their fallen needles there are many shrumps and lumps of mushrooms—from the delicious porcini to the colorful *Amanita muscaria*, which I do not recommend eating! I've found plentiful black trumpets, hedgehogs, and candy caps, and the tawny, prized porcini under pine trees, particularly those entangled with tan oaks in an understory of huckleberry bushes. Many different kinds of pine trees flourish on the West Coast: Monterey and bishop pines, white pines and bristlecone pines and pinyon pine, sugar cone, to name a few. The tree itself is edible in virtually all forms, from the cones to the needles, pollen, and bark. The needles can be a simple tea, the pollen used as flour, and the big pine cones excavated for pine nuts. Italians, Ukrainians, and Russians candy the young green ones in sugar for a piney syrup and chewy, sweet pine candy. One of my favorite parts to forage are the pine tips.

These appear in the springtime as new pale-green growth; they are signs of the tree inhaling carbon from the sky. They have a lemony essence and subtle pine flavor. Douglas fir tips and spruce tips are wonderful as well. In fact, all conifer tips except for the yew tree are edible. They are wonderful as a simple tea or ground up to use as a spice.

PINE CONES

Generally, you want to find these in the springtime when they are very young, soft, and green. Preferably take them from a branch that has recently fallen, or if picking from a tree, just take a few and don't damage the tree. The smaller and fresher the cones, the stronger the flavor will be—so you might want to play with this. Don't use the old, weathered ones sitting under the tree. Those will just break your heart.

Culinarily, you can use pine, fir, and cedar cones; just don't use cypress, hemlock, or anything from a yew.

Piney Ice Cream with Candied Pine Cones

MAKES I QUART, OR 6 TO 8 SERVINGS

½ cup Pine Cone Syrup (recipe follows; requires a month of storage)

6 egg yolks

2 cups heavy cream

1 cup whole milk

Pinch of salt

3 tablespoons pine nuts, toasted

6 to 8 Candied Pine Cones (recipe follows)

This sweet-savory ice-cream recipe allows you to use a couple parts of the pine tree—pine cones and pine nuts. It calls for eggs, so it's actually a creamy, delicious frozen custard. You'll need an ice-cream maker, but you can also wing it and make with a plastic bag, ice, and rock salt. (Find it on the Jerry James Stone website!)

_____

In a medium saucepan, mix the Pine Cone Syrup and egg yolks. Turn the heat on medium-low and whisk in the cream, milk, and salt.

Stir constantly until a creamy, custard-like consistency forms.

Remove from the heat and let cool. Refrigerate the mixture overnight.

The next day, use an ice-cream maker to make the ice cream.

After the ice cream is thick and creamy, scoop into small bowls and garnish with a Candied Pine Cone and toasted pine nuts.

MAKES ABOUT 2 CUPS

2 cups young green pine cones (8 to 12, depending on size), washed and wood ends snipped off

2 cups turbinado sugar

PINE CONE SYRUP

You need about a month for this syrup as the sugar has to dissolve into a thick amber liquid. It's worth the wait, as it will be infused with a complex flavor that tastes of the forest and sunshine and patience. Pine Cone Syrup can be used similar to honey or maple syrup—poured onto waffles and pancakes, swirled into yogurt, served on a cheese plate, or used in a cocktail or soda.

_____

In a clean, dry glass jar, pack the pine cones. ⟶

Cover with the sugar, put a lid on, and shake. Store in a dry place for at least a month for the sugar to break down into a liquid. If it's not happening, place it in a sunny spot. Remove the lid on occasion and let the pine cones breathe so they don't ferment.

When all the sugar has dissolved, strain out the pine cones. These can be used to infuse vodka if you like, or just compost them.

Store the syrup in a lidded glass container in a dry cupboard for up to a year.

CANDIED PINE CONES

*MAKES ABOUT
3 CUPS*

2½ cups small green pine cones, washed and wood ends snipped off

2 cups maple syrup

These should be soft, sticky pine cones that you can pop in your mouth and eat. Right after you make them, the pine flavor can be intense. They make an amazing garnish on soft cheese, or dotted on oatmeal, or placed in the center of thumbprint cookies.

In a small pot over medium-high heat, bring 4 cups of water to a boil. Add the pine cones. When the resin floats to the top, skim it off and continue boiling, about 10 minutes.

Strain out the water, discard, and set aside the boiled pine cones. Add 4 cups of fresh water to the pot and bring to a boil. Return the pine cones to the pot and boil for another 10 minutes. Scoop off any resin. Strain the pine cones and set aside.

Repeat this process a third time. Scoop, strain, and for the final time, let cool and soften.

In a saucepan over medium-high heat, add the pine cones and the maple syrup and bring to a boil for 5 minutes. Then simmer on low for 20 minutes.

Store with syrup in a clean, lidded jar in a cool, dry place.

Pine Scones with Huckleberries

MAKES 8 WEDGE
SCONES

FOR THE SCONES:

⅓ cup pine nuts

1½ cups fresh
huckleberries

1½ cups plus 1 table-
spoon all-purpose
flour, divided

1 teaspoon baking
powder

¼ teaspoon kosher salt

¾ cup plus 1 tablespoon
heavy cream, divided

2 tablespoons sugar

2 tablespoons pine tips,
finely chopped

FOR THE GLAZE:

½ cup confectioners'
sugar

1 tablespoon unsalted
butter, melted

1 tablespoon plus 1
teaspoon Pine Cone
Syrup (page 155),
optional

1 tablespoon water,
divided

One day, while gathering huckleberries on the way to a swimming hole, my friend Maude proposed huckleberry scones—we would just need a few cups, she said. That way, we could stop picking and go swimming. She conceived of a recipe using huckleberries, pine tips, and pine nuts to make for a woodsy "ecosystem-based scone." The pine syrup glaze adds more sweetness and a little more of the ecosystem.

You can make these into savory scones by omitting the huckleberries and using ½ cup of an aged cheese like asiago or Parmesan, reducing bake time by 5 minutes, skipping the glaze, and finishing with the Porcini and Pine Tip Salt (page 168). If you're taking these camping, bake ahead and store the glaze in a separate container and glaze just before serving.

TO MAKE THE SCONES:

Preheat the oven to 425 degrees F.

In a small skillet, toast the pine nuts and then let them completely cool.

In a small bowl, toss the huckleberries in 1 tablespoon of the flour so they don't bleed into the scones.

In a large bowl, mix 1½ cups of the flour, baking powder, and salt.

In another small bowl, mix ¾ cup of the cream and sugar.

Slowly pour the cream and sugar into the dry ingredients, mixing until there's no loose flour left. When close to blended, it will be a little crumbly but should stick together; start folding in the toasted pine nuts, pine tips, and huckleberries, making sure not to overwork the dough.

Using your hands, work the dough into a ball.

Lightly flour a surface and put your dough onto it.

Flour a rolling pin and gently roll the dough into a circle, stopping when it's a smidge under an inch thick. Slice with a knife like a pie into eight wedges.

Put the wedges on a baking sheet lined with parchment paper, and brush the tops with the remaining tablespoon of cream.

Bake for 25 minutes. The tops should be golden brown and the interior moist but not doughy. You may have to sacrifice one wedge to check the center. Note they can easily get dry if overcooked.

Let cool on a cooling rack.

TO MAKE THE GLAZE:

In a small bowl, sift the confectioners' sugar until it doesn't lump— you'll be happy later. Drizzle in the melted butter and pine syrup. Add a teaspoon of water and continue stirring. Add more water until it's the consistency you like. Stir until smooth.

Glaze the scones as soon as they cool.

Piney Chartreuse Swizzle

MAKES 1 DRINK

1½ ounces (3 tablespoons) green chartreuse

½ ounce (1 tablespoon) Pine Cone Syrup (page 155)

¾ ounce (1½ tablespoons) fresh lime juice

1 ounce (2 tablespoons) pineapple juice

Grated nutmeg, for garnish

1 fresh mint leaf, for garnish

My friend Emile came up with this recipe—it's a play on the chartreuse swizzle, a cocktail that bartender Marcovaldo Dionysos introduced to San Francisco cocktail culture in 2003. Chartreuse is an herbal concoction originally made by French monks who played fast and loose with botanicals, adding over one hundred flowers and herbs to this leaf-colored elixir. The pineapple and lime of the swizzle gives it a bit of a tropical feel. By adding pine cone syrup, it taste as green as it looks. Chartreuse has something of a cult following these days and can be hard to find, so you can substitute nocino from page 180.

––––––––––––––––––––––––––––

Fill a Collins cocktail glass with ice.

In a mixing glass, combine the chartreuse, syrup, lime juice, and pineapple juice. Pour into the cocktail glass.

Garnish by sprinkling nutmeg and floating the mint.

TIPS, NEEDLES, AND NUTS

Pine needles are edible, and if you're marooned somewhere and suffering from a bout of scurvy, by all means, make teas, tinctures, and salads from mature pine needles. The older the needles, the more vitamins and nutrients. However, as they mature, their flavor is also stronger and tastes more like cleaning fluid. Dried pine needles are great for starting fires, and both these and dry pine cones added to a fire you're cooking on can add a delightful essence. There's also a recipe in the Coast section wherein you cover mussels with dried pine needles and set them on fire to impart their fabulous flavor (Flaming Pine Needle Mussels, page 43).

But if you're going for flavor and versatility, then pick the young pine, fir, or spruce tips. These are lemony with just a hint of pine resin in them. They're highly versatile as well. I blend them into salt (page 168), dry them for teas, pickle them (page 164), ferment them, and use them in the spice blend when making Sockeye Salmon Gravlax (page 165). Pick a few from a tree and move on, then pick a few from another tree. You won't hurt the tree, unless you pluck from the very top, and then it's believed the tree will grow misshapen.

Many edible nuts are out there! Acorns have long been a staple for Indigenous peoples in Northern California. Despite their availability and health benefits, I've found them to be a huge amount of work, and sometimes I still can't get the bitter tannins out. Oregon grows 99 percent of the hazelnuts in the United States! But that's not the case near where I live. So I encourage you to forage for nuts and find ways to use them. The two included here—bay laurel and green walnuts—are bountiful in the woods and city streets not far from me, and the recipes for them are relatively simple.

Pickled Pine/Spruce Tips

MAKES 2
8-OUNCE JARS

2 lemon slices

2 bay laurel leaves

1 teaspoon pink
peppercorns

2 cups fresh, young
spruce or pine tips

½ cup water

½ cup apple cider
vinegar

1 tablespoon sugar

1 tablespoon kosher salt

These have a lovely lemony, conifer flavor but a woody, waxy texture, so chop them into pieces and sprinkle onto Mushroom Pâté with Wine-Soaked Walnuts (page 100). If making a rillette from wild salmon or black cod, add these pine tips cut up. When serving bagels with Sockeye Salmon Gravlax (page 165), these are an unexpected and delightful addition, either blended with cream cheese or used as a garnish instead of capers.

In each of two clean and dry jars, add a lemon slice, 1 bay laurel leaf, ½ teaspoon pink peppercorns.

Remove any woody pieces from the tips. Rinse if necessary. Pack 1 cup of the tips into each jar.

In a small saucepan over medium heat, add the water, vinegar, sugar, and salt. Stir until the sugar and salt dissolve.

Pour the pickling liquid into the jars. Make sure the tips are entirely covered.

Cover the jars and store in a cool, dry place. Give them a week or so before tasting. They'll keep for a year in the cupboard.

Spruce Tip and Juniper Berry Sockeye Salmon Gravlax

**MAKES 12 TO 15
SERVINGS**

2 sockeye salmon fillets,
frozen, skin on (1 to 1
½ pounds each)

1 cup kosher salt

1 cup turbinado sugar

1 cup fresh spruce tips

½ cup juniper berries

¼ cup freshly ground
black pepper

The flavor and scents of spruce and juniper in this recipe remind me of my time spent on the exquisite Kachemak Bay, Alaska. The combination of the two trees also happens to taste like gin. If that's your thing.

There's no food that lifts spirits, triggers the kundalini, or hits all the pleasure centers like wild salmon. I love nothing more than breaking down a whole fish and using every part—but the fillets I'll save for gravlax. It's ridiculously easy, much easier than smoking fish. First, always use frozen salmon fillets or freeze your own fillets overnight wrapped in plastic. Salmon are wormy fish and should not be eaten raw. If you're freezing fillets longer than overnight, then vacuum-seal them to avoid freezer burn. Serve alongside Pickled Pine/Spruce Tips (page 164) with soft chevre and whole grain wheat toast or bagels.

———————————————

Remove the sockeye fillets from the freezer and thaw.

In a food processor or spice grinder, mix all the dry ingredients. If you live in a cabin in Alaska with no electricity, then chop up the spruce tips and juniper berries and mix with the salt, sugar, and pepper. (No need to fire up the generator for this.)

Lay the salmon fillets on a baking sheet, skin side down. Rub the dry mix over both fillets, making sure to evenly coat them.

Wrap each fillet in plastic and add something heavy on top to weigh them down. You can use clean rocks, a thick book you didn't love, or a heavy pan.

Store the whole contraption in the fridge or a cool place for 5 days, then scrape the rub off and cut into thin slices before using.

Pine and Porcini Crackers

MAKES 6 TO 8 LONG, RECTANGULAR OR 25 TO 30 SMALLER TRIANGULAR CRACKERS

1½ cups all-purpose flour

½ teaspoon salt

4 teaspoons porcini powder

3 teaspoons pine tips, finely chopped

½ cup water, plus more as needed

3 tablespoons extra-virgin olive oil, divided

1 tablespoon Porcini and Pine Tip Salt (recipe follows)

Crackers are fun to make, and you can put all manner of herbs, seeds, seaweed, and edible flowers into the dough for creative crackers. Or you can put salts tarted up with wild ingredients on plain crackers for a little extra something-something.

Along with including pine tips and porcini powder in the cracker dough, I also like to finish these crackers with the Porcini and Pine Tip Salt (page 168). But you can always use plain finishing salt.

Preheat the oven to 450 degrees F.

In a mixing bowl, blend the flour, salt, porcini powder, and pine tips.

Add the water and 2 tablespoons of the oil to the dry mix and blend until there's no dry flour left. If it feels really dry, add a little more water a few tablespoons at a time.

I like to roll my cracker dough out through a pasta maker. To do this, I cut it into four sections and pound each one out into a rectangular or oval shape and run it through the highest setting. I then lower the settings and run it through again. I lower the settings again, and roll it through again. I do this until I have the thinnest-possible dough that isn't yet broken.

If you don't have a pasta maker, knead the dough 12 to 20 times and then, using a floured rolling pin and parchment paper, roll it out until you get it as thin as possible. ⟶

You can make large crackers people will crack apart or slice the dough into rectangles or triangles, brush with the remaining oil, and sprinkle with the finishing salt. Press the salt into the dough lightly so it sticks.

Bake for 8 to 10 minutes. The crackers should be crispy but not burned, so check on them on the early side.

PORCINI AND PINE TIP SALT

MAKES ABOUT ¼ CUP

¼ cup flaky sea salt

1 tablespoon porcini powder

1 tablespoon pine tips, finely chopped

If you have some subprime porcini, or just some dried porcini and some pine (or fir) tips that should be used, this salt is a great way to incorporate them into a finishing salt that adds a woodsy accent for savory dishes.

In a clean 4-ounce jar, mix the flaky salt with the porcini and pine tips.

Store in a cool, dry place.

Douglas Fir G & T

MAKES 1 COCKTAIL

1 cup sugar

1 cup water

½ cup fresh young
   Douglas fir tips

2 ounces gin

Tonic water

This is my sister Betsey's recipe. She's a master gardener and forager and a bit of a cocktail maven. Her new favorite gin is Roku, but she also suggests St. George Terroir Gin for this. The recipe makes more fir tip simple syrup than you need for one cocktail, but chances are it'll go quickly once you (and your friends) taste this herbaceous gin and tonic.

TO MAKE THE SIMPLE SYRUP:

In a small saucepan with a lid, heat the sugar and water until the sugar is dissolved.

Remove from the heat and add the fir tips. Put in a clean jar or cover the pan with the lid, and leave them at room temperature for at least 3 days.

Strain the simple syrup into a jar and keep refrigerated.

TO MAKE THE COCKTAIL:

In a mixing glass, combine the gin and a tablespoon of the simple syrup. Pour over ice in a highball glass and add tonic to taste.

BAY LAURELS

Bay laurel nuts are a recent discovery for me, and I'm obsessed with them. They appear in the fall under bay laurel trees—small drupes, or avocado-like nuts—ranging in color from pale green to purple, depending on their ripeness.

These nuts can be gathered off the ground and then taken home and peeled and dried. They can last for years like this. When you're ready to use, roast them. Their scent while raw is herbal and foresty, but after they've been toasted in the oven, they smell nutty and warm but are still very perfumy. They will have an intense flavor like cacao or coffee. I like to grind up the roasted bay laurel nuts and add some to my morning coffee for a little warmth.

DIY: "Lost in the Woods" Bitters

MAKES ABOUT 1½ CUPS

3 wild cherry plums, with pits

2 bay laurel leaves

1 (1-inch) piece of reishi mushroom, or 1 teaspoon dried reishi powder

2 turkey tail mushrooms, or 1 teaspoon dried turkey tail powder

1 tablespoon pink peppercorns

1-inch piece of pine bark, or 1 teaspoon pine bark powder

2 cups grain alcohol or high-proof vodka

Get inspired for these medicinal bitters after a hike; here we are going for a fruity, peppery, herbal, and bitter liquid that you can add to cocktails or put a dash or two into soda for a low-alcohol, adaptogenic aperitif. All of the ingredients can be dried and stored for later use.

_____

In a clean 16-ounce jar, add all the ingredients, then cover with a lid and shake.

Store for a month in a dry, cool place. After a month, strain and bottle the liquid. (If you want the flavor more intense, just infuse it longer.)

Bay Laurel Nut Hot Cocoa

MAKES 4 CUPS

4 tablespoons roasted, powdered bay laurel nuts (from 15 nuts, peeled)

4 cups coconut milk (or half-and-half, or your preferred nondairy milk)

1 tablespoon cacao, unsweetened

1 tablespoon orange zest (from about 1 orange)

½ teaspoon dried rose petals, finely ground

¼ teaspoon cinnamon

1 to 2 tablespoons sugar (optional)

12 Bay Laurel Marshmallows (recipe follows) or store-bought (optional)

Using bay laurel nuts in a rich, thick, semisweet hot cocoa reminds me a bit of the Mexican warm beverage *champurrado*, which is a hot chocolate thickened with masa harina, or corn flour. Cacao is typically a little bitter and not as sweet as hot chocolate. There are a lot of flavors going on here that you don't want to drown with too much sugar, so taste first and add sugar to your liking. When camping, I mix all the dry ingredients together and just spoon them into the coconut milk as I'm heating it up. You can use other milks, but I find coconut has a natural sweetness to it. And all the nondairy milks have different consistencies—I like using a thick, creamy one, rather than a watery one for this recipe. I suggest making larger batches rather than smaller ones and saving the bay laurel nut powder in a jar.

Preheat the oven to 350 degrees F.

On a baking sheet, place the bay laurel nuts in a single layer and roast for 30 minutes. Move them around on the sheet, and return to the oven for another 30 minutes to an hour. They're done when they're a toasted caramel color. Remove from the oven and let cool.

Using a nutcracker, or something that works as one, crack the shells and remove the meats.

In a spice grinder, grind the roasted nuts until fine—they'll be a bit sticky from all the nut fat. Lay them out on a sheet and when dry, grind them again until they are powder.

In a medium saucepan over low to medium heat, warm the coconut milk and add the powdered bay laurel nuts and remaining ingredients except the sugar. Taste and add a little bit of sugar, but don't add so much you lose the subtle flavors. ⟶

Continue to cook over low heat, stirring so that it doesn't scorch on the bottom of the pan, about 5 minutes. It may be a little gritty, so strain before serving if you like.

Top with the marshmallows.

BAY LAUREL MARSHMALLOWS

MAKES 40 ½-INCH OR 20 1-INCH MARSHMALLOWS

1 cup room-temperature water, divided

3 envelopes (about ¾ ounce) unflavored gelatin

1 teaspoon kosher salt

2 cups sugar

1 cup light corn syrup

2 teaspoons finely ground dried bay laurel leaf (use a spice grinder for this, then sift out any stems), divided (optional)

1 teaspoon vanilla extract

Coconut oil spray (for greasing the pan)

1 cup confectioners' sugar, plus more for dusting

1 teaspoon cornstarch

Marshmallows got their name from the marshmallow plant, as the root of the plant was originally used in making these. This plant has all sorts of medicinal and healing properties. Modern-day marshmallows do not. But I still make them, as they are lots of fun and there is something about a crackling fire that just calls for their sweet-sticky presence on your fingers and lips. Homemade marshmallows are far better than store-bought in taste and texture and you can flavor them with just about anything—from borage flowers and wild mint to bourbon and butterscotch to chai and hibiscus. For this recipe, I use dried and ground bay laurel leaf and vanilla. You'll need a candy thermometer and a stand mixer. Try the marshmallows atop the Bay Laurel Nut Hot Cocoa (page 173) for an immersive, bay laurel sensory experience. This recipe makes far more than you will use on the hot cocoa recipe, so bring your sharpened sticks for roasting.

Once you master the craft of marshmallow making, you can use ingredients like real marshmallow root and agave. I don't plan on ever mastering the craft of marshmallow making, so I keep it simple and janky and use corn syrup, which prevents the crystallization of the sugar at high temperatures.

_____

In the bowl of a stand mixer, combine ½ cup of the water, the gelatin, and salt. Stir and let sit. This is known as "blooming" the gelatin.

In a large saucepan on medium heat, add the remaining ½ cup of water, sugar, and corn syrup and stir to blend as you bring it to a boil. Since the temperature will need to rise above boiling, use a candy thermometer to measure the temperature. It will take 7 to 9 minutes to get it to 240 degrees F. It should be a firm ball. Drop in a little cold water to test readiness—if it forms a firm but pliable ball, it's done.

In the stand mixer on low, mix the gelatin. With the mixer running, slowly pour the hot sugar mixture over the gelatin. Increase the mixer speed to high and let it beat for about 8 minutes.

Add 1 teaspoon of the bay laurel powder and the vanilla and keep beating for 2 more minutes. The mixture will increase in volume as the bowl fills up with a mound of shiny and thick white fluff.

Grease a 9-by-13-inch pan with coconut oil and spread the marshmallow mixture in the pan. For thinner marshmallows, spread on a baking sheet.

Let the marshmallows cool for 3 hours or overnight.

Taste to see if you like the bay laurel flavor as is, or if you want to include more. It's a very strong flavor and can easily overwhelm.

In a shallow bowl, combine the confectioners' sugar, cornstarch, and if you wish, the remaining 1 teaspoon bay laurel powder.

Spray coconut oil on the knife for cutting them so they don't stick.

To slice, use a cutting board and dust it with confectioners' sugar, then remove the sheet of marshmallows from the pan and place it on the cutting board. Dust the top with confectioners' sugar and cut them. It's much easier than trying to do it in a pan.

Drop each one into the confectioners' sugar mix to keep them from sticking together. They will be very tacky to the touch until coated.

Store in an airtight container at room temperature for up to 2 months. These do not keep in the fridge or freezer.

GREEN WALNUTS

It was hard to decide whether to put this in the Urban section or in the Forest section of this book. Walnut trees are large and formidable, but you're much more likely to come across green walnuts in someone's backyard or in an urban park than hiking in a patch of woods. While California does have a species of native black walnut, *Juglans californica*, most of the time the trees we get green walnuts from are English walnuts, or *Juglans regia*, which are used more in landscaping. Make sure to harvest green walnuts in spring or early summer, before they get too hard.

One afternoon in early May, I was meeting with a private client, Lenny, in Sonoma wine country. We were going over the dinner menus for a weeklong Cyclepalooza he hosts and I noticed that workers were trimming a beautiful tree right over his outdoor table—not far from the wood-burning pizza oven. The branches on the ground were laden with green walnuts. I cut off a bunch of the sticky green orbs, the size of Ping-Pong balls, took them home with me, and immediately started the nocino process. It can take up to two months minimum to make, and the people would arrive to cycle through wine country in just eight weeks. So I had to get to steeping.

I decided to break it out on pizza night, when the wood-fired oven would still be hot. Stone fruits were in all their glory at the farmers' market, so I caramelized some in the oven and then served them over vanilla ice cream with drizzled nocino on top. This dessert was served to the diners under the mother walnut tree whose branches spread luxuriously above the table. It's become a summer tradition, and our signature dessert for Cyclepalooza.

Nocino-Drizzled Caramelized Stone Fruit over Ice Cream

MAKES 10 SERVINGS

3 pounds mixed stone fruits (such as 3 yellow peaches, 4 firm plums, 6 apricots)

½ cup unsalted butter

¼ cup sugar

2 quarts high-quality vanilla ice cream (such as Straus)

2 cups Nocino, for drizzling (recipe follows)

Grilling stone fruit—whether at home, in a wood-fired pizza oven, or outdoors on a campfire—takes these summertime jewels to the next level. They get even sweeter and their flavor intensifies. You'll want to use fruit that is just ripe—but not too ripe and soft as it will just disintegrate in the heat. When choosing which stone fruit to roast, I generally go for yellow peaches and nectarines over white ones as they have a heartier flavor. Apricots of all types have a certain sorcery when cooked, and plums cook fast and can collapse into heaps of jammy goodness, but are still worth including. The drizzle of nocino adds warm spices and a bittersweet accent to the dessert.

Make a fire and let the wood burn down to a low flame, just before coals. Set up a large cast-iron skillet over the fire.

Wash and cut the fruit in halves and remove the pits.

In the skillet, melt the butter and then sprinkle the sugar evenly over the bottom of the pan.

Lay the fruit pit side down in the butter and sugar. Cover with aluminum foil (if using an oven, you don't need the foil) and cook for 10 to 15 minutes. Check with a fork—the fruit should be soft all the way through.

Remove from the heat and set aside until cool enough to handle. Then remove from the pan and slice each half into about four pieces.

Scoop the ice cream into bowls and top with the fruit, making sure to give each a variety of all three. Then drizzle with nocino and serve!

**MAKES ABOUT
1 LITER**

25 to 30 young green
walnuts, washed and
quartered

1 cup sugar or maple
syrup

2 sticks cinnamon

7 whole cloves

1 vanilla bean, split
lengthwise

1 tablespoon lemon zest

1 liter vodka or grain
alcohol

NOCINO

This wouldn't be a proper foraging book without a recipe for a liqueur made from green walnuts. In France it's called *liqueur de noix*, in Italy they make a version called *nocino*, and in Spain it's *ratafía*. It's a simple green-walnut infusion that makes a festive dark-brown liqueur that virtually nobody drinks for some reason. (If you ever see someone in a bar order a nocino and tonic, please let me know.) It can taste a bit like a Christmassy Jägermeister—herbaceous with a lot of warming spices. It's a lovely digestif straight, but if you drizzle it over ice cream, people really love it. Glove up for this, as the walnuts stain hands, shirts, and cutting boards a brown-chartreuse color.

In a large clean jar, add the walnuts, sugar, spices, and zest.

Pour in the vodka and screw a lid on the jar. The vodka will turn milky green, but it eventually becomes brown.

Shake the jar to help the sugar dissolve. Set on a counter where you will see it and remember to give it a shake, or turn it upside down every day, or at least frequently. Let steep for at least 2 months and up to a year. It will darken in color over time, the tannins from the nuts will mellow, and the liqueur will be smoother the longer it ages.

To bottle, strain out the walnuts, return the liqueur to the clean jar, cover, and store in a cool, dry place.

FIDDLEHEAD FERNS

Fiddleheads of ferns, also known as crosiers, are as lovely as they are delicious, with a fractal pattern like the spiral end of a fiddle. These are the new starts of the beautiful fern swords that sprout every spring. These delicacies have a narrow window, maybe a few weeks. They're crunchy and taste like asparagus and sometimes artichokes, with a "je ne sais quoi" earthiness to them. Not all ferns are edible; there are about ten thousand varieties of this ancient, beautiful plant, so learn which ones are safe to eat from an expert. I will describe two of the most common and popular.

In Alaska, the most common and safest bet for fiddleheads is the ostrich fern (*Matteuccia struthiopteris*). It has large, long, luxurious plumes that grow from three to four feet in height as if coming out of narrow vases, in clumps called crowns, with about seven plumes in each one. Ostrich ferns are also easy to identify in fiddlehead form. Their stems are smooth and green and have a deep U-shaped groove on the inside of the stem. Their fiddleheads are covered with papery brown sheaths. They're always smooth and never hairy, like some other species of ferns.

When foraging for them, never take more than one fiddlehead per bunch so the plant can flourish year after year. Snap it off with your hand so you don't nick the other stems with a knife or scissors and accidentally harm them. Harvest before the fronds start unfurling.

In the Pacific Northwest and California, look for lady ferns (*Athyrium filix-femina*). Lady fern fiddleheads have many similarities to the ostrich fern. They grow in clusters with five to eight swords, which resemble luxurious feather boas that stretch up to six feet tall. A unique characteristic these ferns have are diamond-shaped blades as opposed to triangular-shaped like the bracken fern. In spring, when just breaking ground, they also have a papery brown substance covering the fiddleheads that will need to be scraped off before using culinarily.

Wilted Greens, Wild Onions, and Fiddlehead Ferns

MAKES 2 MAIN COURSES OR 4 SIDE DISHES

2 tablespoons unsalted butter or olive oil, plus more as needed

1 bunch thick asparagus, trimmed, cut in half, and shaved (if using thin asparagus, slice into rounds)

2 cups pea shoots (or 1 cup chopped greens)

¼ pound fiddlehead ferns, boiled for at least 5 minutes

4 wild onions (ramps or wild leeks), including bulbs and flowers, washed and chopped (save the flowers for garnish)

2 cups spring greens (such as lamb's quarters or chard), chopped into bite-size pieces

½ teaspoon kosher salt

¼ teaspoon freshly ground black pepper

¼ teaspoon Aleppo pepper

2 tablespoons fresh lemon juice

Finishing salt

Early spring has such a sense of green bursting forth with new life. This dish is pure green-on-green springtime. Serve over blue polenta and add a poached egg or some Lemony Salt-Preserved Anchovies (page 80), or serve it alongside wild rice and a piece of roasted halibut. You can also use it as the basis of a frittata.

———————————————————

In a skillet on medium-high heat, melt the butter or the olive oil. Add the asparagus and cook for just under a minute, then add the pea shoots, fiddleheads, and onions. Stir, adding more oil or butter if needed.

Then add the greens, salt, pepper, and Aleppo pepper, stir, and turn off the heat.

Toss with the lemon juice.

Plate and garnish with onion flowers and finishing salt.

Pickled Fiddleheads

**MAKES ONE 16-
OUNCE JAR**

1 heaping cup fiddle-
head ferns

1 cup apple cider
vinegar

1 cup water

1 tablespoon kosher salt

1 tablespoon sugar

1 cup ice water

1 garlic clove

½ teaspoon black
peppercorns, whole

Due to their short season, fiddlehead ferns are frequently pickled. They can also be stir-fried, deep-fried, sautéed—*just don't eat fiddle-heads raw!* They can really mess with your stomach. So I recommend thoroughly blanching them by cooking for a minimum of five and up to twelve minutes before doing anything with them. Their taste is sort of like broccoli's feral cousin with the crunch of raw asparagus. Use these for a tempura-fried fiddlehead fern, add them to cheese platters with crostini and morel mushrooms, or make savory tarts with them. (Note: due to blanching, pickled fiddleheads can go soft, so I recommend using within a week or so.)

Clean all the papery brown casings off the fiddleheads. Set aside.

In a saucepan over medium heat, mix the vinegar, water, salt, and sugar until everything is dissolved. Let cool to room temperature.

Bring a large pot of water to a boil, then add the fiddleheads and blanch for 5 to 12 minutes. Put them in an ice-water bath immediately so they stay green and firm. Drain and put in a clean glass canning jar.

Pour the vinegar mixture over the fiddleheads. (There may be a little extra brine, but make sure to fill to the top so all the fiddleheads are covered.)

Add the garlic and peppercorns.

You can preserve the pickled fiddleheads for months in the canning jar, or use them within a few days.

FOREST GRAZING BOARD

THE
URBAN

EDGE AND FORAGING

PEA SHOOT

FAVA LEAVES

STINGING NETTLES

MUSTARD

URBAN FORAGING GEAR LIST

- Comfortable but fashionable shoes
- Shoulder bag or backpack
- Clean scissors or small garden pruners

WHERE TWO ECOSYSTEMS OVERLAP IS KNOWN as the "edge" or the "fringe" in permaculture. These areas often have the most diversity and richness; they've got friction, which heightens their creative power. These are the liminal spaces where life transforms. The edge is also where human ecosystems and nature overlap—a large urban park surrounded by dwellings and where suburbs meet the countryside. These are places of dappled light and shade, of new ecosystems forming. It's in these margins that riches are found. And it's here that we can tap into our feral selves, even if just for small bursts like an evening walk.

Nature is persistent, even in urban spaces. Trees sprouting through cracked cement, mushrooms growing at their bases, and birds and bees pollinating all the fruits and flowers. But on a deeper level, nature is everywhere because it's carried within us. Most people are just a few generations away from ancestors who lived rurally and had to know the seasons to eat what they grew or could find. When our people packed up and moved to the city, or to a new country, the landscape remained in the tempo of our music we dance to; it's in the cadence of languages; it inspires architecture and art. And the landscapes of our ancestors live on in our food.

Multicultural urban areas are the ultimate edge, where many cultures overlap and new fusions are constantly born. Urban foraging is rich with surprises. Since the core components of this final section come from urban foraging, wild greens, flowers, and fruit figure most prominently. So enjoy the shifting of seasons by snipping cherry blossoms, learning to love feral fennel, and finding salad fixings in sidewalk cracks. The grazing board for this section showcases desserts. I find that at some gatherings, people like to get up and move around for dessert, so a grazing board offers small, more varied options.

Wild Greens

RALPH WALDO EMERSON DESCRIBES A WEED as "a plant whose virtues have not yet been discovered." There is a gap in seasons where the winter vegetables and fruits are over and the summer ones have yet to appear, let alone ripen. It's in this crevice between seasons that wild greens appear, harbingers of new life pushing up through the dirt. These beckon us to stoop down and notice their nuanced, modest presence. They may be sour or bitter or very grassy. When picking them, they may sting or be sticky. Wild greens are to butter lettuce like the wolf to your domesticated dog. Sometimes it's nice to have a little of both the intense wild and dumbed down in a salad.

So when making a salad from super-nutrient-dense dandelion and fava leaves, add some butter lettuce or Little Gems. Or sweeten it up with some beets, add in pickled foods for crunch and a delicious dressing to pull it all together. And all those lovely little flowers appearing on the wild radish and feral mustard are great garnishes. Wild greens often have only a short window when they can be enjoyed. Once past their prime, they can be tough and inedible. So get them while they're young!

Along with salads, soups are where you can let your creativity shine. There are very few rules—in fact, soup making is the opposite of baking. It does not require precision and is very forgiving. If you don't like how it tastes, keep flavoring and tasting.

You can also use wild greens in savory tarts, frittatas, stir-fries, and about anything else you would use regular greens in. You just need to spend a little time down on the ground getting to know them.

GETTING TO KNOW YOUR WILD GREENS

Miner's Lettuce

FLAVOR: mild with a slight tanginess

BEST IN: salads

ABOUT: Lore has it that gold miners ate this lettuce to keep from getting scurvy as it grows plentifully and is rich in vitamin C. It grows from Alaska to Central America. It appears in the spring as heart-shaped green leaves and then grows into round disks with a tiny white flower in the center. As it gets older the texture is denser and crisp, but the flavor stays mild and tangy.

Lamb's Quarters

FLAVOR: very mild, similar to chard or a very flavorful spinach

BEST IN: salads and soups; highly versatile

ABOUT: This stuff grows everywhere—literally you'll find it coming out of cracks in sidewalks and appearing as weeds in your container garden. Gather it from places where dogs can't get to. (Note: Lamb's quarters have oxalic acid when raw, so eat in moderation. When cooked, this is not an issue. Avoid the seeds.)

Dandelion

FLAVOR: bitter

BEST IN: salads

ABOUT: Most of our grocery-bought salad greens have had the bitter bred out of them, with iceberg being popular for its watery crunch and absence of flavor. On the other end of the spectrum are dandelions, which are an unapologetic, bitingly bitter experience. But don't let this scare you off. They have forty times more bio-nutrients than iceberg lettuce and eight times more antioxidants than spinach. You just need to find the best ways to use them.

Wild Arugula

FLAVOR: spicy, peppery

BEST IN: salads, pesto

ABOUT: The leaves of this green are best in the spring, before they become too spicy and tough. But later in the year, their flowers are great garnishes for salads and soups and their seedpods can be pickled.

Fava Leaves

Fava plants replenish the soil by adding nitrogen, as well as support diverse microbes in the dirt and suppress weeds, so many permaculture and organic farmers and gardeners use it as a cover crop. These crops tend to jump the perimeters and grow feral, so one of my favorite places to forage for fava leaves is in the ditches near permaculture farms.

FLAVOR: mild, grassy, earthy, savory

BEST IN: sautés, pesto

ABOUT: Pick the youngest, freshest leaves—usually from the top of the plant, as they can get tough and have an unpleasant mouthfeel when older. They're silvery and gray green. I really love fava—the leaves, flowers, and later the beans are all edible and taste like spring.

Pea Shoots

FLAVOR: crisp, tangy, sweet

BEST IN: salads when young, or stir-fries and steamed for older leaves

ABOUT: Pea shoots are also used to replenish the soil, so you'll often find shoots in these same edges, along with wild radish and fennel. I've got a hot spot I hit in the spring that has all these along with feral mint.

Chickweed

FLAVOR: mild, sweet

BEST IN: salads and garnishes

ABOUT: It's all over the place and it looks a bit weedy—with lots of small green leaves and a modest white flower. It's very versatile but delicate when young so doesn't hold up terribly well in soups or when stir-fried.

Sorrel

FLAVOR: sour, lemony

BEST IN: salads and soups

ABOUT: Many varieties exist throughout the United States. It has cloverlike leaves and grows small pods. The ones near me have bright-yellow flowers. There's also lovely violet wood sorrel that has a lavender underside to its leaves and light-purple flowers. It's often invasive, which does no good to local fauna, so eat away!

Purslane

FLAVOR: lemony, crunchy, green apple-ish, hint of pepper

BEST IN: soups, stews, salsas, and salads

ABOUT: Purslane is a delicious succulent that makes me think of Greek islands—even though I've never been to one, to date. It was used by ancient Greeks as a cure for "female troubles." It's also commonly found in Middle Eastern dishes. It's low to the ground and has small leaves that grow in clusters of five or six, and has hairless, plump leaves, both small and larger. It's drought-hardy and likes poor soil and neglect. And it's a super-food nutrition-wise, with omega-3 fatty acids and lots of vitamin C.

Watercress

FLAVOR: peppery, spicy, bright

BEST IN: atop flatbreads, wilted in soups, stir-fried à la mustard greens, or raw in salads

ABOUT: Watercress can be found in streams and growing along springs. (Make sure the water source does not have any livestock or toxic industries nearby.) It grows from the stream to above the water's surface. Pick the new growth above the water surface. It has smaller leaves than store-bought watercress and makes three to five oval-shaped leaflets.

Stinging Nettles

FLAVOR: inky, peppery, like spinach on steroids

BEST IN: pesto, pasta dishes, on pizza, sautéed, as a base for soups (never raw in salad)

ABOUT: As their name implies, these sting when picking, so always wear protective gloves when handling them. When you get home, bring water to a boil, drop them in for about a minute or two, then drain and run them under cold water. This way, they won't sting and still keep their deliciousness. They can also be frozen and used later. Make sure they are thoroughly cooked before eating them.

Miner's Lettuce, Pea Shoot, and Pickled Herring Salad

*MAKES 4 APPETIZERS
OR 2 MAIN COURSES*

1 blood orange, pithed, peeled, and either left as wedges or chopped into ¼-inch pieces

1 Cara Cara orange, pithed, peeled, and either as wedges or chopped into ¼-inch pieces

2 cups miner's lettuce

2 cups romaine lettuce, chopped

1 small head speckled or red leaf lettuce, torn into bite-size pieces

½ cup Lemon-Mint Yogurt Dressing (recipe follows), plus more for drizzling

4 fillets of Blood Orange and Meyer Lemon Pickled Herring (page 72)

Wild onion blossoms (optional)

Herring arrive in late winter and early spring to spawn on the eelgrass of the intertidal zone. They provide food for so many creatures of the bay so that come spring, they will be fat, healthy, and fertile. They are pre-spring, or what I call the "fertile void." There will still be citrus falling from trees or at your farmers' market and grocery store. And miner's lettuce and wild onions out yonder in the hills.

_____

Set a few of your most beautiful pieces of citrus aside.

In a large bowl, add the greens with the remaining citrus pieces and dressing. Toss until everything is covered.

Plate and then add the pickled herring and citrus slices over the top of the greens. Drizzle more dressing over the herring.

Garnish with the wild onion blossoms.

¾ cup whole milk plain
yogurt

Zest and juice of 1
lemon

10 to 12 mint leaves,
torn into small pieces

1 tablespoon white
wine vinegar or white
balsamic

2 medium garlic cloves,
minced

½ teaspoon cumin
powder

½ teaspoon kosher salt

LEMON-MINT YOGURT DRESSING

Early spring in my neighborhood, mint seems to sprout in wild, random patches and trees are dripping with Meyer lemons. I love this dressing for springtime salad with wild greens.

_____

In a blender, combine all the ingredients.

Let sit in the fridge for at least 1 hour, or overnight. Enjoy on salad!

Wild Green Savory Galette

*MAKES 6 TO 8
APPETIZER SERVINGS
OR 4 MAIN COURSES*

FOR THE CRUST:

¾ cup all-purpose flour,
plus more for rolling
out dough

½ cup spelt flour

½ cup (1 stick) unsalted
butter, very cold
and diced into small
pieces

¼ cup plus 1 tablespoon
ice-cold water

1 teaspoon kosher salt

This is a simple stunner that makes good use of wild greens and those that are in your crisper that need to be used. Almost any type of wild green can be used here: fava leaves, dandelion greens, spring pea, arugula, stinging nettles; and mix in some kale, beet greens, chard—anything goes. The recipe calls for green garlic, which is milder than garlic cloves, so reduce the amount of garlic accordingly if using cloves. This is also good finished with a sprinkle of Porcini and Pine Tip Salt (page 168). I personally love to put blue cheese on these tarts and let it bake into the greens, but I know there are a lot of strong feelings about blue cheese.

If you want to make this super simple, buy a frozen pie crust or use phyllo dough that doesn't need melted butter spread between all the layers.

TO MAKE THE DOUGH:

In the bowl of a food processor, add the flours and butter and pulse until it beads and resembles coarse sand.

Add the water and salt, and pulse until the dough starts to come together. Remove and form it into a ball.

Wrap the dough in plastic and put in the fridge for at least an hour. You can also make several of these and freeze them for up to a month.

When ready to make your galette, flour a surface and a rolling pin.

Place the ball of dough onto the floured surface and whack it a few times to flatten it out. Then roll it into a circle until it's about ⅛ inch thick.

Transfer to a baking sheet, leaving about an inch hanging over the sides. Set aside.

FOR THE FILLING:

3 tablespoons unsalted butter

1 yellow onion, sliced in half-moons

¼ cup green garlic, diced, or 2 garlic cloves, finely minced

6 cups mixed wild greens (such as fava leaves, arugula, or stinging nettles), roughly chopped

3 tablespoons extra-virgin olive oil

1 tablespoon fresh thyme

1 teaspoon kosher salt

1 teaspoon freshly ground black pepper

1 cup grated Parmesan cheese, plus ¼ cup more for sprinkling

1 egg yolk, beaten with 1 teaspoon of water

1 teaspoon flaky sea salt

TO MAKE THE FILLING:

In a large skillet over medium heat, add the butter. When it melts, add the onions and cook until translucent.

Add the garlic and cook for a few minutes, stirring so nothing burns.

Add the greens, drizzle with the oil, and season with thyme, salt, and pepper. The greens will cook way down. You don't want to put them on the crust with too much moisture, so make sure it has cooked out. When they are wilted, turn off the heat.

Sprinkle the 1 cup of cheese over the bottom of your pie crust.

Lay the greens in the center of the crust and spread them out, leaving about 2 inches around the diameter with no filling.

Fold the crust up, overlapping as you go.

Sprinkle the rest of the cheese or whatever else you like over the greens.

Brush the top and sides of the crust with the egg wash. Sprinkle the flaky salt over the crust.

Bake for 30 minutes.

Wait until it's just cool enough to not burn your mouth before eating. This will make you happy on a rainy day.

Chilled Springtime Soup

MAKES 4 APPETIZER SERVINGS

3 cups mixed wild greens (like miner's lettuce, sorrel, arugula, chickweed)

2 cups plain Greek yogurt

1 cup water

½ cup blanched fresh peas

Juice of 2 lemons (about ¼ a cup)

2 tablespoons fresh basil, chopped (about 6 leaves)

2 tablespoons fresh mint, chopped (about 10 small to medium mint leaves)

1 clove garlic, finely minced

1 teaspoon lemon zest

1 teaspoon kosher salt

½ teaspoon cumin

½ teaspoon freshly ground black pepper

2 tablespoons toasted walnuts, chopped, for garnish

Extra-virgin olive oil, for garnish

Red wine vinegar, for garnish

Sorrel flowers, for garnish

Finishing salt

This soup tastes like a fresh spring meadow, or a side yard someone forgot to mow—in the best possible way. It's tart, tangy, garlicky, and refreshing. The flavors should make you want to dance a wee jig. If you use regular yogurt instead of Greek, wait until after you blend it all to add the water—you may not need it.

Puree all the ingredients except the garnishes. Chill overnight or up to 3 days.

To serve, put into four bowls and drizzle olive oil over the soup, add a few drops of vinegar, and sprinkle with walnuts, flowers, and finishing salt. Serve immediately.

Watercress, Purple Potato, and Wild Leek Soup

MAKES 4 APPETIZER SERVINGS

2½ cups Mushroom "Bone" Broth (page 96) or chicken broth

3 cups diced purple sweet potato (see note)

1 cup roughly chopped white onion

2 tablespoons plus 1 teaspoon extra-virgin olive oil (such as Olio Nuovo) divided

1 cup sliced leeks, white and light green parts only

1 teaspoon kosher salt

½ teaspoon freshly ground black pepper

½ teaspoon red chili flakes

1 cup watercress

Seaweed Salt (page 83) or flaky sea salt, for finishing

Purple sweet potatoes like Stokes Purple or Okinawan give this recipe a sweetness that nicely contrasts the spicy watercress. Try this with the Seaweed and Citrus Salad with Mulberry-Kombu Vinaigrette on page 23 for some powerful color contrasting.

In a medium saucepan over medium heat, add the broth and potatoes and cook for about 6 minutes. The potatoes should be soft.

In a medium skillet over medium-high heat, add the onions and 2 tablespoons of the oil and cook until translucent, about 3 minutes.

Add the leeks and sauté. When they are cooked through and the edges are golden, add them to the pan with the potatoes and broth.

Season with the salt, pepper, and chili flakes.

Using an immersion blender, puree the soup. You can make it extra smooth or leave it a little chunky. Don't overmix as it can become glue-like.

In a small bowl, add the watercress and drizzle with the remaining 1 teaspoon oil. Toss until evenly coated.

Divide soup in bowls and top with the watercress and Seaweed Salt.

Note: If you can only find orange sweet potatoes, use half sweet potatoes and half white potatoes as the orange kind tends to be sweeter than the purple varieties.

White Bean Stew with Stinging Nettles and Oyster Mushrooms

MAKES 4 SERVINGS

2 cups oyster mushrooms, divided

¼ cup extra-virgin olive oil, plus more as needed

½ cup chopped white or yellow onion

1 clove garlic, minced

5 cups Mushroom "Bone" Broth (page 96) or vegetable broth

1 cup dried white beans (such as gigantes or corona), soaked overnight

1 (2-inch) piece of kombu

½ teaspoon kosher salt

½ teaspoon freshly ground black pepper

½ teaspoon red chili flakes

3 cups stinging nettle leaves and chopped stems

Flaky sea salt, for finishing

The beans matter. My favorites are *gigantes* that I get from Iacopi Farms at my local farmers' market or the Royal Corona bean from Rancho Gordo. These both are creamy, meaty, and flavorful and unlike beans in a can. As my sister once wisely pointed out, "If you aren't buying a lot of meat, you can afford the good beans." And if you get the good beans, you won't miss meat.

Oyster mushrooms have a mild, savory flavor. I set aside the smallest, prettiest ones for a crispy topping; they can get soggy in a soup. The other oyster mushrooms you can chop up and sauté with the onions; they add bulk and flavor but don't create a funky texture. Stinging nettles are a righteous addition to this, with their inky-green magic. If you don't have these, other leafy greens will work.

Shred and dice 1½ cups of the larger oyster mushrooms. Set aside the smaller ones.

In a large pot or Dutch oven over medium-high heat, add the oil and onions and sauté until translucent.

Add the mushrooms and garlic to the onion mixture and cook for a few minutes.

Pour in the broth and add the white beans, kombu, salt, pepper, and chili flakes.

Simmer on medium-low for 40 minutes. Check and stir on occasion to make sure the white beans are submerged.

Add the stinging nettles and cook for a few minutes.

Take the smallest oyster mushrooms or most pristine shredded mushrooms, about ¼ cup, and sauté them in olive oil or butter until crispy and golden. Add a pinch of salt.

Scoop the white bean soup into bowls with a slotted spoon so that you get more solids than liquid.

Top with the crispy mushrooms and a sprinkle of finishing salt. Note the white beans will absorb more liquid as they sit in the broth, so I like to let them bathe in it to get plumper and tastier.

~~~~~~~~~~~~~~~~~~~~~~~~~

Delectatio: the surge of delight and joy
we feel when we experience beauty.

—JOHN O'DONOHUE, *BEAUTY:*
THE INVISIBLE EMBRACE

Stinging Nettle Gnocchi with Brown-Butter Black Trumpets

MAKES 4 APPETIZER SERVINGS OR 2 MAIN COURSES

FOR THE GNOCCHI:

16 ounces whole milk ricotta cheese

1 egg

¾ cup all-purpose flour, plus more as needed

1 cup grated Parmesan, Romano, or pecorino cheese

1 teaspoon kosher salt

4 cups loosely packed stinging nettles

The rich, truffly, slightly smoky flavor of the black trumpet means that it doesn't need much added to be delicious. Gnocchi is a perfect foil for it—soft and mild with some butter and cheese. Keep the dish simple and let the trumpets shine.

I really love black trumpets and stinging nettles together. They both share an inkiness; the trumpets are earthy, the nettles grassy. In a pinch, make this with reconstituted dried black trumpets by soaking them in hot water for thirty minutes. Black trumpets are also great with sage, so if you don't have stinging nettles, you could add these fresh herbs to the gnocchi.

_____

TO MAKE THE GNOCCHI:

In a large bowl, mix the ricotta and egg. Add the flour, Parmesan, and salt. Stir until just combined.

Bring a large pot of water to a boil. Add the stinging nettles, stir, and quickly drain. Rinse with cold water, then chop into small pieces when cool enough to handle. With your hands, or the back of a large spoon, squeeze the excess moisture from the nettles.

Add the stinging nettles to the dough. If the dough feels wet, add a tablespoon of flour at a time until it can be formed into a ball. The dough should be sticky. ⟶

½ cup plus 1 tablespoon
unsalted butter,
divided

1 tablespoon extra-
virgin olive oil

1 pound black trumpet
mushrooms (or 2
cups dried), cleaned

1 medium shallot, diced

¼ cup warm water

Kosher salt

Freshly ground black
pepper

2 tablespoons roughly
copped toasted
walnuts

2 to 4 tablespoons
grated Romano,
Parmesan, or
pecorino cheese

Flour the counter and scrape the dough out onto it. Cut the dough
into four pieces. Working with one piece at a time, roll the dough into
a rope about an inch thick and cut into bite-size pieces. Repeat this
process, placing the gnocchi on a floured baking sheet. (At this point,
the gnocchi can be kept covered in the fridge for up to a day, or you
can freeze it.)

Bring a large pot of salted water to a boil. Make a swirl in the water with
a large spoon to help keep the gnocchi from sticking. Then drop the
gnocchi in the water quickly so they cook at about the same time—you
may do this in two batches, depending on the size of the pot. Boil the
gnocchi until they float to the top and are cooked through, about 4
minutes. Drain.

TO MAKE THE BLACK TRUMPET SAUCE:

In a large skillet on medium-high heat, add a tablespoon of the butter
and the oil.

Add the mushrooms and shallots, stir for about a minute, and then add
the water. Cook the mushrooms and shallots until the water evaporates.
Continue cooking for another 5 to 10 minutes, or until the shallots are
golden brown. Season with salt and pepper and remove from the heat.

In a frying pan over medium heat, add the remaining ½ cup butter. Swirl
the pan occasionally. As the butter melts, it will begin to foam. Continue to cook, swirling the pan occasionally, until it turns from yellow to
golden to, finally, brown, about 8 minutes.

Add the mushroom mixture to the brown-butter sauce and toss lightly.

In a shallow serving bowl, add the gnocchi—they are delicate, so don't
handle them too much after they've been cooked.

Pour the black trumpets, onions, and butter over the gnocchi, and carefully toss. Sprinkle with the walnuts and Romano cheese and serve.

Peak Summer Purslane and Farro Salad

MAKES 4 SERVINGS

1 cup dry farro (will make 2 to 3 cups cooked farro)

4 cups purslane, torn into bite-size pieces

2 cups cucumber, chopped into ¼-inch cubes

1 cup heirloom tomato chopped into ¼-inch cubes

½ cup goat cheese, crumbled

½ cup Preserved Lemon and Anchovy Dressing (recipe follows)

2 tablespoons sunflower seeds, for garnish

Purslane likes summer heat and so do tomatoes and cucumbers, so make this hearty grain salad in the peak and late summer months. It can be packed to go for picnics and camping trips in a cooler and served at room temperature.

———————————————

Cook the farro according to the directions on the package. Different types of farro will have varied cooking times. Rinse after cooking.

In a large bowl, add the purslane, cucumbers, tomatoes, goat cheese, and the cooked farro. Toss with the dressing.

Divide into bowls and garnish with the sunflower seeds.

½ cup neutral-flavored oil (like avocado)

½ cup extra-virgin olive oil

¼ cup preserved lemon peels (page 212)

¼ cup water

4 fillets from the Lemony Salt-Preserved Anchovies (page 80), or 2 store-bought anchovy fillets

PRESERVED LEMON AND ANCHOVY DRESSING

This recipe calls for home-preserved anchovies, but feel free to use the tinned ones—just fewer of them, since home-preserved anchovies are much less salty. If you're vegan/vegetarian, you can easily substitute two cloves of fermented black garlic for the anchovies.

In a blender, emulsify all the ingredients. If too thick, add more water.

Enjoy on salad!

10 lemons

1 cup kosher salt,
   divided

PRESERVED LEMONS

In my section of a California, lemons thrive in the foggy, never too-cold or hot microclimates. People rich in lemons give them away by the bulging bagful. If you're a luck recipient of these, making preserved lemons is a great way to use them. They are usually Meyer lemons, which are less sour than true lemons and have thinner skins, but they work as well. Once you have these they quickly become staples. These come from Northern Africa originally and are used in Moroccan tagines.

Choose the four best-looking lemons and slice off the tips where the branches held the lemons, and then slice them into six segments, but don't cut all the way through; they should stay attached at the base.

Sprinkle salt between the segments and add 2 tablespoons of salt to the bottom of a jar.

Juice the remaining lemons.

Put the segmented lemons (and I use some of the rinds from the juiced lemons) into the jar, pressing them down so they all fit.

Cover them all with lemon juice. You may need to juice more lemons.

Shake the jar every few days.

These are salt and acid, so don't need to be refrigerated, but will last longer if you do so.

Wild Berries and Fruit

WHEN I'VE PUBLISHED ARTICLES ABOUT FORAGING fruit in urban areas, inevitably, there's always an outraged commentator: "You should never take fruit from private or public property. It's illegal!" Outrage! Rather, presumably, it should be allowed to fall onto sidewalks or into gutters and streets to ferment until the rainy season comes and washes them away. And then another commentator chimes in about how they own a fruit tree and every year, just as the fruit ripens, thieves arrive in the night and steal everything. This is how far from nature we've gotten. Rather than assume raccoons and other critters ate their fruit, which is most likely the case 99.9 percent of the time, they believe someone is casing their tree and arriving with night goggles and a ladder to steal every single piece of fruit. And then these criminal masterminds are presumably making vats of jam with all that fruit. Come on, people on Nextdoor: nobody is stealing your fruit.

Branches hanging over sidewalks are considered public property—so it's perfectly legal to forage from these but a good practice to ask homeowners anyway.

WILD BERRIES

Come summertime, it's hard to find a place on the West Coast that does *not* have berries growing. You'll find huckleberries in the understory of a forest or someone's backyard. Salmonberries grow on the tundra and in spruce forests or hanging over the deck of a farmhouse on Lummi Island or off a trail in Alaska. Blackberries are everywhere. Look for them alongside the parking lot at your local library, a highly trafficked walking path, the chain-link fence of an abandoned lot. Wet boggy areas are rich in blueberries, while raspberries can grow in full sun or semi-shade and take over whole fields; there are red and black currants, cranberries, Aronia berries, and wild, small, sweet strawberries up on the ridge—always remember, even when times are tough, that you are rich in berries.

Wild Berry Galette

FOR THE CRUST:

1 cup cold butter (2 sticks), cut into little pieces

2½ cups all-purpose flour, plus more as needed

1 tablespoon sugar

1 teaspoon kosher salt

½ cup ice-cold water, plus more as needed

2 egg yolks, divided

Splash of fresh lemon juice

FOR THE FILLING:

6 cups mixed berries (such as blackberries, salmonberries, or huckleberries)

3 tablespoons honey or your preferred sweetener

1 tablespoon cornstarch

Zest of 1 lemon

This is a favorite hands-on activity at Wild Food Camp Alaska. Everyone gathers mounds of the sparkling, jewel-like berries and we all make easy, beautiful, and delicious rustic galettes from them. Pie making is more of a science; galettes are more of a craft. Participants tend to make their galettes in all manner of shapes; some garnish theirs with edible flowers, others with a simple egg wash or sprinkle of sugar. Think of your galette as your canvas and the shape and character an expression of your whimsical self.

The pie crust is inspired by Homer, Alaska's delightful Two Sisters Bakery. You can also buy premade crust from the grocery store and then this recipe will take less than fifteen minutes to assemble. But you will lose all cred from bakers for buying your pie crust. I have been shamed many times for the premade crust, but I still do it on occasion.

TO MAKE THE CRUST:

Cut the cold butter into the flour, working the mixture with your hands and rubbing between your fingers. When it is well combined, add the sugar and salt and mix.

Add the water, 1 egg yolk, and lemon juice to the flour mix and work to form a ball of dough, using more flour or water as needed to keep it from being too dry or sticky.

Wrap tightly and refrigerate for an hour, or up to a week. (You can also freeze the dough for up to a month.) ⟶

TO MAKE THE GALETTE:

Preheat the oven to 375 degrees F.

Cut the pie dough in half, roll back into balls, and place on a well-floured surface.

Using a well-floured rolling pin, roll the pie doughs out into a circle, or let them form whatever shape you'd like.

Transfer the pie dough rounds onto a baking sheet lined with parchment paper.

In a large bowl, add the berries, honey, cornstarch, and zest. Gently combine, making sure most of the berries are left whole.

For most galettes, you'd place the filling in the center and then fold the edges up and around it. But so the berries don't roll around, you could fold up the pie dough first, leaving a 2–inch border, then pour the berry filling in the middle, mounding slightly.

Mix the remaining egg yolk with 1 teaspoon of water and brush on the tops of the crusts.

Bake for 30 to 40 minutes, or until the crust is golden brown and the berries are bubbling.

Wild Berry and Peony Pavlova

*MAKES ONE 8-INCH
ROUND OR SIX
2-INCH ROUNDS*

FOR THE MERINGUE:

3 large egg whites

½ teaspoon cream
of tartar

Pinch of salt

½ cup superfine or
castor sugar

1 tablespoon cornstarch

FOR THE TOPPING:

1½ cups heavy cream

1 teaspoon pure vanilla
extract

2 cups fresh berries

¼ cup fresh or dried
peony petals

Berry pavlovas are one of my favorite summertime desserts. They're light and beautiful and showcase seasonal fruit at its peak. These fluffy meringue desserts are named for a famous Russian ballerina, Anna Pavlova—the meringue is made to be in the shape of her tutu. But I wouldn't sweat the tutu shape your first time trying this. And why not add the delicately fragrant peony petals?

Peonies are not wildflowers in Alaska, but Alaska, it turns out, is one of the few places on earth where peonies bloom in July. The pink Sarah Bernhardt, a fragrant, double-petaled bloom, is one of the most popular. They're everywhere in Homer: farmers' market vendors sell them by the bucketloads, people have overflowing vases in their homes, and even the Salty Dawg Saloon often has these beauties poking out of mason jars. So let's use a few. Though not from the Salty Dawg.

TO MAKE THE MERINGUE:

Preheat the oven to 200 degrees F.

In a large mixing bowl or stand mixer on medium-high speed, beat the egg whites with the cream of tartar and salt until soft peaks form.

Gradually add in the sugar and cornstarch to the forming peaks with the mixer still running, until thickened and shiny.

Line a baking sheet with a piece of parchment paper, and fold the meringue onto it in about an 8-inch circle, or in six 2-inch circles.

⟶

Bake the large meringue for 2 hours; bake the small circles for 1 hour. Turn off the oven with the door closed. Leave the meringue in the oven for at least an hour, or as long as overnight.

Your pavlova can last for up to 2 days at room temperature.

TO MAKE THE TOPPING:

In a large mixing bowl or stand mixer, add the cream and vanilla and whip until it's thick and custard-like.

In a small bowl, gently combine the berries and most of the peony petals, reserving about a quarter of the petals for garnish.

Remove the meringue from the baking sheet very carefully and put on a platter.

Spread the whipped cream on the center of the pavlova. Top with the berry-peony mixture.

Sprinkle the remaining peony petals over the pavlova and onto the plate.

Serve in large scoops, making sure there's meringue, cream, and berries in each serving.

Salt-Fermented Blueberries

MAKES ONE 16-OUNCE JAR

2 cups blueberries

Non-iodized salt

If you have a lot of berries, one way to preserve them is to ferment them with salt. Lacto-fermented blueberries are sour and somewhat savory. They can be added to salads and yogurt or oatmeal, or pureed to make mocktails or cocktails or sauces. These were popularized by the famous Copenhagen restaurant Noma and, as they tout them, blueberries require little prep and freeze well. Here's a simple version.

Weigh your blueberries. Measure the salt to 2 percent of the weight of the blueberries.

Mix the ingredients in a bowl, then transfer them to a clean, dry quart-size jar.

Put a two-piece lid on the jar, loosely sealed, or use a fermentation cap.

Keep in a cool, dry place—not the fridge. The warmer the weather, the faster these will ferment.

In 5 days, taste the blueberries. They should be complex, sour, a little herbal, and effervescent.

Store in the fridge for up to a week or freeze, tightly wrapped.

Chilled Huckleberries with Campfire Caramel and Seaweed Salt

MAKES 6 TO 8 SERVINGS

1 (14-ounce) can sweetened condensed milk

6 cups huckleberries or other slightly tart berries, chilled

1 teaspoon Seaweed Salt (page 83)

While traveling in Lapland, the northern part of Finland, I had a dessert that's stayed in my memory. It was chilled lingonberries served with warm caramel. It had all the sensations: sugary and sour, warm and cold. I loved it. Tart wild berries like huckleberries, blueberries, and currants would all work well. And the caramel here is a hack I learned from the chef Beverly Torrez-Petty at our Wild Mushroom Camp at Camp Earnest in the Sierra Foothills. She inherited it from her mom. As Beverly warned, and I can't overcaution, if not done correctly, a can of sweetened condensed milk can turn into a bomb. You can easily make this on the stove top as well, but it is an easy, fun camp-side dessert.

Make a fire and let the wood burn down to a medium flame. You may need to feed the fire. Set up a large pot filled with water over the fire.

Put the can of sweetened condensed milk into the pot, making sure it is covered with water. Boil for 2 hours, and it magically becomes caramel. However, if the waterline goes below the top of the can, it can explode. *So the can must always be submerged.*

Carefully remove the can from the hot water with tongs. Using a can opener and a towel to protect yourself from the heat, remove the top of the can, and voilà! It's warm, delicious caramel.

Fill bowls with the chilled tart berries, top with warm caramel, and sprinkle with seaweed salt. Serve immediately.

Fermented Blueberry and Goat Cheese Salad with Fall Greens

MAKES 4 APPETIZER SERVINGS

4 cups Little Gem lettuce

2 cups fall greens, like wood sorrel or watercress

½ cup Salt-Fermented Blueberries (page 223) or other fresh berries, divided

⅓ cup Stinging Nettle Vinaigrette (recipe follows)

4 ounces fresh goat cheese, cut into 4 rounds

⅓ cup chopped and toasted walnuts

2 teaspoons Truffle Honey (page 142) or regular honey

I love this salad. It's inspired by the Dordogne region of France, which was once the epicenter of truffle cultivation in France; it was known as the Périgord region, and the famed truffle still has this name. They cultivate walnuts there and are known for their Rocamadour goat cheese, a phenomenally fresh, young cheese. Most of the salads I had there were topped with a generous slice of this goat cheese and a sprinkle of toasted walnuts, and the dressings were made with walnut oil rather than olive oil, giving them a nutty, deeper tone. This recipe calls for stinging nettle–infused vinegar, which is a perfect foil for the walnut oil. A drizzle of Truffle Honey over this cheese will land your senses right in the French countryside.

In a large bowl, toss the greens and ¼ cup of the blueberries with the Stinging Nettle Vinaigrette.

To plate, top with the goat cheese rounds and sprinkle with walnuts and the remaining blueberries. Drizzle with truffle honey.

¾ cup walnut oil

¼ cup Nettle-Infused
   Vinegar (variation
   below)

1 small shallot, finely
   minced

1 teaspoon Dijon
   mustard

1 teaspoon fresh thyme

¼ teaspoon kosher salt

¼ teaspoon freshly
   ground black pepper

STINGING NETTLE VINAIGRETTE

Walnut oil has a buttery, nutty flavor, and stinging nettle vinegar tastes grassy and tart. You can use either of these main ingredients in a variety of salad dressings, and they also work well together.

In a blender on high speed, add the ingredients and mix to emulsify.

VARIATION: NETTLE-INFUSED VINEGAR

Fill a jar with stinging nettles and then completely cover them with white balsamic vinegar. Put it in the cupboard and forget about it. It can be used as soon as 2 weeks or left for up to 6 months. The flavor does get stronger over time, so taste and strain out the nettles when you're satisfied.

Raspberry and Chamomile Jam

**MAKES ONE
6-OUNCE JAR**

2 cups raspberries

⅔ cup sugar

2 tablespoons fresh
lemon juice

4 tablespoons cham-
omile, dried and
ground

2 teaspoons chia seeds
(optional)

Raspberries have gone wild in and around Homer, Alaska. Along hiking paths and sidewalks, these unruly bushes get thick with fruit in
late summer. One day, when I was out picking them, I kept coming
across little patches of chamomile, also known as pineapple weed.
I picked some and tossed it into my bucket of berries. It became
inseparable in the jumble, and so I made a raspberry and chamomile
jam and loved it.

Yet when I see the ratio of sugar to berries that jam recipes call
for, I hesitate a bit. You may as well be eating hard candy. Sugar
helps to preserve and thicken jam, so when I make mine with far less
sugar, I use it more as a thick sauce or add a small amount of chia
seeds to thicken it. This jam is a bit tart and very raspberryish, while
the chamomile adds a lovely harmony to it.

In a medium saucepan over medium-high heat, add the berries, sugar,
and lemon juice. Bring to a boil.

Simmer and add the chamomile, stirring well, for 10 minutes. Turn off
the heat and stir in the chia seeds.

Let cool, then transfer to a clean 6-ounce jar.

Store in the fridge for a few weeks. Or water-bath can for longer-term
storage.

Blackberry and Elderflower Compote

MAKES 2½ CUPS

1 pint blackberries

½ cup Elderflower and
Lemon Simple Syrup
(page 249)

One morning, while cooking at a house out in the countryside, I was simmering some blackberries for a compote and happened to see elderflowers in bloom outside the window. So this recipe also happened. Initially, I just added the elderflowers to the blackberries, but since the elderflowers have a short season and are delicate, it's more practical to make the Elderflower and Lemon Simple Syrup first. This compote is great mixed into overnight oats or chia seed pudding, or atop pancakes, over ice cream, or swirled with plain yogurt.

___

In a small saucepan over high heat, bring the blackberries and simple syrup to a boil.

Simmer on low for 30 to 45 minutes.

Remove from the heat and use right away, or let cool and place into a 16-ounce mason jar. If you plan on storing the compote, give it a water bath by placing the jar in a large baking dish and pouring boiling water around it so it comes halfway up the sides.

Blackberry del Bosque Mocktail

MAKES 4 MOCKTAILS

2 tablespoons honey

¼ cup warm water

1½ cups fresh blackberries

3 limes (juice from 2; wedges from 1)

1 teaspoon finely ground salt

⅛ teaspoon sumac

Pinch of red chili flakes

Ice

2 tablespoons "Lost in the Woods" Bitters (page 171)

2 cups sparkling water

This one went through multiple rounds with my friends and recipe tasters Tania and Martin. It's very purple and fruity but not sweet.

Melt the honey in the warm water. In a blender, add the melted honey, blackberries, and lime juice and puree.

On a small plate, mix the salt, sumac, and chili. Run a wedge of fresh lime around the rims of the glasses. Dip them into the salt mixture and fill the glasses with ice.

In a mixing glass, combine the blackberry juice, bitters, and sparkling water, or mix very gently in the glass.

Garnish each glass with a wedge of lime and a sprig of mint.

VARIATION: MAKE IT A COCKTAIL

Make the recipe as written, but add 1½ ounces of gin and 1½ ounces of *amaro* such as Amaro Nonino or St. George Bruto Americano.

LOQUAT

Another common but often ignored fruit in my town is loquat. Loquat trees are originally from China and were brought here as ornamentals, valued for their leathery deep-green leaves. In Chinese medicine, it's believed that the fruit and leaves are good for sore throats, respiratory problems, and digestion. Their fruit is a washed-out mustard yellow, and they often have brown spots, so they aren't the prettiest to behold. Yet their scent is wonderful and you'll most often smell fragrant bunches of loquats before you see them. Of course, forage from private property only if you have permission. If not, stay on the sidewalks or in public spaces. But this is a fruit virtually nobody uses. It grows in clusters that are easily snipped off trees.

Once home, quickly wash and deseed them. Put the seeds in a colander to wash all the meat off, and reserve them for Loquat Seed Liqueur (page 234). The flesh you can make a *mostarda* from or simply toss into your rum pot (page 238).

Loquat Sour

MAKES 1 COCKTAIL

1½ ounces Loquat Seed Liqueur (recipe follows)

4 teaspoons (⅔ ounce) Candy Cap–Infused Bourbon (optional; page 147)

1 ounce fresh lemon juice (from about half a lemon)

1 teaspoon simple syrup

2 dashes "Lost in the Woods" Bitters (page 171) or Angostura bitters

Ice

1 maraschino cherry, for garnish

Lemon peel, for garnish

The liqueur made from loquat seeds is much like amaretto, which is made from apricot pits. This has a nutty, savory aroma and flavor, perfect for a foraged version of an amaretto sour.

In a shaker, mix the liqueur, bourbon, lemon juice, simple syrup, and bitters without ice for 15 seconds.

Add the ice and shake for an additional 30 seconds.

Strain into a highball glass (the foam will collect on the top).

Garnish with the cherry and lemon peel.

LOQUAT SEED LIQUEUR

MAKES 2 CUPS

2 cups loquat seeds, rinsed and dried in the sun for 2 weeks

2 cups vodka

1 vanilla bean, split lengthwise

2 to 4 strips of lemon peel

½ cup simple syrup

The classic Italian recipe calls for grain alcohol, but a neutral vodka works just as well. It has a lovely fruity, earthy fragrance with amber tones to it. Use this any way you would amaretto. This takes a month or longer to make, so be sure and plan ahead.

Once the loquat seeds have dried out, add to a mason jar with the vodka, vanilla bean, and lemon peels.

Let sit for 2 weeks to a month.

Strain out the seeds and compost.

Add the simple syrup to taste and enjoy.

WILD CHERRY PLUMS

The diminutive plums that come from *Prunus americana* trees ripen in the SF Bay Area in the peak summer months. You may feel them squish beneath your feet as they fall to sidewalks or notice birds looking particularly full and satisfied as they reel between the trees. If so, look closely at the overhanging trees. These plums are not a highly valued fruit, as they tend to be much smaller than cultivated ones; they're about the size of a cherry and with a flavor that's far more tart.

I have a dog-friendly walking trail near my home that literally becomes a wild plum forest in the summer. I find small burgundy plums, white and yellow plums that are a bit larger, and even some feral large plums, presumably planted by the Portuguese dairy farmers who homesteaded the area decades ago. Even though wild cherry plums are plentiful, they take time to clean and pit, so keep in mind that you are facing a lot of work processing them and that the birds like them too.

Wild Cherry Plum Compote

2 cups ripe wild cherry plums, pitted

½ cup elderflower honey

1 medium fresh or dried California bay laurel leaf, or 2 dried Mediterranean bay leaves

Juice from half a lemon

Elderflower honey gives this compote its floral essence, but you can use regular honey if you prefer. At this honey-to-berry ratio it will still be very tangy. I prefer this recipe less sweet as you can taste the flavors and the compote will be more versatile. Swirl this plum compote along with some tahini into plain yogurt. Top with torn fresh mint and black sesame seeds for a tasty and beautiful breakfast. It also makes a great filling for homemade Pop-Tarts.

In a saucepan on medium-high heat, add all the ingredients and bring to a light boil.

Simmer on low for an hour, stirring occasionally.

Pick out the bay leaves.

Let cool before pouring into a glass jar for storing.

Keep refrigerated. Use within 2 weeks, or try water-bath canning for longer storage.

DIY: Rum Pot

MAKES 2 QUARTS

**Fruit you have too much
of or no idea what to
do with**

**About 2 cups straw-
berry tree berries
(see note)**

Turbinado sugar

**1 (750 mL) bottle dark
rum,**

If you've got some loquats that don't look pretty or too many cherry plums, or you're not sure what to do with tree "strawberries" or pineapple guava, simply put them into a rum pot. (Known in Germany, where it's believed to have originated, as *rumtopf.*) The fruit gets all boozy and the booze fruity. You can just keep adding more fruit and sugar and let them stew as it's more of an infusion than a fermentation. The idea is that fruit is added throughout the summer and fall, and it's ready just in time for visitors during the December holidays, or for solo drinking in the glow of holiday lights.

In a pot that holds at least 2 quarts, layer the firmest fruit on the bottom. Sprinkle some sugar over it. Then layer more fruit and more sugar.

Pour the rum over it.

All the fruit should be submerged. If it's not, weigh it down with a plate. Put a lid on the pot. It's not fermenting, so it doesn't need to get air. Keep in a cool, dark place in your house.

You can add more fruit, sugar, and rum as suits you over the next 3 to 4 months. Move to a larger container if need be.

Strain out the fruit to serve the rum either warm or cold. Use the fruit to make a rum cake, rum balls, rum milkshakes, or cocktails.

Note: This ornamental "strawberry tree," similar to the Pacific madrone, is actually the Mediterranean *Arbutus unedo*. It dangles and then drops its fruit flagrantly around city and suburban scapes. They are round, gooey red fruits with tiny seeds inside. The taste is sweet and somewhat strawberry-like, while the texture is not as enticing as that of a strawberry. I enjoy eating them fresh, but can be at a loss as to what to make from them. Then I remembered the rum pot.

Grandma Mabe's Rum Pot Cake

MAKES 1 CAKE

FOR THE CAKE:

Butter spray for pan

1 box yellow cake mix (no pudding)

1 box instant vanilla pudding

4 eggs

½ cup canola oil

½ cup water

½ cup Rum Pot rum (page 238)

½ cup walnuts, chopped

12 rum-soaked strawberry tree berries from the Rum Pot (page 238)

This book's photographer, Marla Aufmuth, developed this recipe with her rum pot–soaked strawberry tree berries and a cake that lives large in her holiday tradition. It's an adaptation of a cake made by a woman she describes as "not my grandma, but she was awesome as grandmas should be. The first time I went to the South, I was served a rum cake at Grandma Mabe's house. I fell in love with it and have made it every year since. It's a lovely way to celebrate the holidays." She uses the cake mixes and boxed pudding that Grandma Mabe used to excellent outcomes, so here it is, adapted with foraged fruits and pine needles.

TO MAKE THE CAKE:

Preheat the oven to 350 degrees F.

Grease a Bundt pan with butter cooking spray, making sure to coat all the nooks and crannies.

In a large bowl, add the cake mix and instant pudding, crack the eggs into the middle, and mix well. Stir in the oil, water, and rum until all the ingredients are mixed. Fold in the walnuts.

Pour the batter into the prepared pan. With a butter knife, make holes to drop the strawberry-tree berries into the batter. They will sink as the cake bakes, so make sure they are covered up with the batter. Add all the berries in various spots around the cake.

Bake for 50 to 60 minutes until the top looks golden brown. Insert a toothpick into the thickest part of the cake; it is done when the toothpick is dry or just a few crumbs are attached.

Let the cake cool in the pan on a rack. $\longrightarrow$

FOR THE DRIZZLE:

½ cup Rum Pot rum
   (page 238)

¼ cup sugar

FOR THE GLAZE:

1 cup confectioners'
   sugar

2 tablespoons unsalted
   butter, melted

2 to 4 tablespoons milk
   (or hot water), for
   desired consistency

½ teaspoon vanilla
   extract

Pine tips for garnish

TO MAKE THE DRIZZLE:

In a small saucepan over medium-high heat, warm the rum and sugar until the sugar is dissolved.

Once the cake is cool, use a skewer to poke holes at different depths and pour the drizzle into the holes. Let the cake sit for 3 hours to absorb the drizzle.

Remove the cake from the pan by turning the pan upside down on a plate and gently tapping until it releases.

TO MAKE THE GLAZE:

In a large bowl, add the confectioners' sugar, butter, 2 tablespoons of the milk, and vanilla.

Mix until it becomes a glossy finish. Add more milk (or water) until it is the desired consistency. It should be thick enough to sit on top of the cake and drip down the sides.

Using spoonfuls, drizzle the glaze over the cake. Garnish with the pine tips.

Ponche Navideño

MAKES 12 CUPS

10 cups water

1 cone of piloncillo (pure cane sugar) shaved, or 1 cup brown sugar

⅓ cup dried hibiscus flowers

2 cinnamon sticks

5 whole cloves

1 tablespoon tamarind paste

Juice of 1 lemon

Juice of 2 oranges

2 cups Rum Pot rum with fruit (page 238)

Lemon slices, for garnish

My brothers all married women who are from Mexico. Christmas holidays at the border city of El Paso with my very large, extended, Irish Mexican family involves vats of tamales; platters of crisp, sweet *buñuelos*; and a large pot of warm *ponche* always sitting on the stove with a ladle and cups nearby. This recipe uses the ponche as a base, but then ramps it up with the Rum Pot fruit and rum.

_____

In a large pot over high heat, add the water, sugar, hibiscus flowers, cinnamon sticks, cloves, and tamarind paste, and bring to a boil.

Simmer on low for 15 minutes.

Remove the cinnamon, cloves, and hibiscus.

Add the lemon and orange juice and the Rum Pot rum with fruit and stir.

Remove from the heat, divide into cups, and garnish with the lemon slices.

There's a cultural view in which flowers are dainty, trivial, dispensable—and a scientific one in which flowering plants were revolutionary in their appearance on the earth some two hundred million years or so ago, are dominant on land from the arctic to the tropics, and are crucial to our survival.

—REBECCA SOLNIT, "ON THE MYRIAD MEANINGS OF THE ROSE"

WHILE WE CAN SEE THE CATERPILLARS trundling their way up branches, and later witness soaring gossamer butterflies flitting between flowers, what we don't see is the process taking place in the cocoon or chrysalis. This has elicited musings from many a poet and philosopher. Gaston Bachelard wrote, "The word *chrysalis* alone is an unmistakable indication that here two dreams are joined together, dreams that be-speak both the repose and flight of being, evening's crystallization and wings that open to the light." The butterfly emerges from the dissolution of the caterpillar. The butterfly has a critical job to do. It's a pollinator. While feeding from flowers, butterflies get pollen on their legs and transfer it from flower to flower.

A wide array of flowers are edible not only to the butterfly but to humans as well. Though some are not, so make sure you have consulted an expert before eating them. Many flowers are edible, but don't have much flavor and can quickly wilt and turn funky colors. The ones that are most desirable have an array of flavors from spicy, like the nasturtium or wild mustard flowers, to fragrant and floral, like the rose and lavender. You can also use them as herbs and seasonings since they carry a milder version of a plant's flavor, like fennel blossoms or arugula. As garnishes, they make salads and soups prettier, can be the basis of creative cocktails, and add beauty and whimsy to desserts.

ELDER-FLOWERS

The elderberry bush is popular in landscaping, so there's no telling where you will find one of these. Elderflowers appear as modest white clusters of flowers in early spring. Despite their appearance, their scent is shamelessly sweet. Your nose may locate these before your eyes do as the scent travels on the breeze through open windows. When visiting a friend or relative, look alongside their driveway or follow that fabulous smell, and at times you'll encounter entire hedgerows of them. Don't take them all, as the bees and butterflies love them too!

Flowers with the strongest fragrances also tend to have the most flavor. So elderflowers are definitely a top contender. Their flowers are fragile, so you need to either use them right away or dry them for later use. Elderflowers are fine to eat without cooking, but no other part of the plant is edible raw, including the berries. They won't seriously injure you, but can cause stomach problems if you don't boil the berries first.

Ume Plum, Lemon, and Elderflower Tonic

MAKES 1 MOCKTAIL

15 ounces high-quality tonic

2 tablespoons ume plum paste (see note)

¼ cup Elderflower and Lemon Simple Syrup (recipe follows)

Juice of 2 lemons

Ice

This mocktail is a bit like a greyhound, but with a floral essence to it. Ume plum paste has a salty, tart flavor that's fruity without being sweet. I learned of it from my friend and neighbor Tre Balchowsky. She and I designed a dinner event with rituals around the redwoods and salmon. We included a significant hike in and out to the event, so we wanted to limit the alcohol intake but also for people to enjoy a sophisticated mocktail.

In either a blender or shaker, mix all the ingredients except the ice. Make sure the ume plum paste is thoroughly blended.

Serve in highball glasses over ice.

Note: Ume plum paste is a Japanese staple made from fermented ume plums. It's also known as *umeboshi* paste and often available in the Asian foods section of grocery stores. Some DIYers ferment the ume plums themselves with salt and shiso. It's a bracingly tart and salty paste but quickly grows on you.

4 cups water

2 cups raw sugar

1 cup elderflower blossoms (10 to 15 flower heads), picked from the stem and rinsed

2 lemons, zested, sliced, and deseeded

ELDERFLOWER AND LEMON SIMPLE SYRUP

Marla developed this recipe, and she tried it with both sugar and honey but found that the flavor of honey overpowered the flowers, so she went with sugar. Elderflowers are ready when the creamy flowers pop right off. This is delicious added to sparkling water or champagne.

_____

In a medium saucepan over medium heat, add all the ingredients including the lemon zest and give a quick stir.

Bring to a quick simmer.

Remove from the heat and steep, covered with a dish towel, for 24 hours.

Strain out the ingredients, pour into a quart-size jar with a tight lid, and refrigerate.

If tightly sealed, it should keep for a month.

Elderflower French 75

MAKES 1 COCKTAIL

1 ounce gin

1 ounce Elderflower and
Lemon Simple Syrup
(page 249)

Ice

3 ounces sparkling wine
or champagne

Lemon twist, for garnish

The French 75's history harks back to Paris in 1915 when a bartender added a shot of gin and lemon juice to champagne. It made a cameo appearance in the classic film *Casablanca*. It was also regularly featured at my cold-water, SF Bay swimming club at happy hour. Another delicious addition to sparkling wine is elderflower cordial, so this has a lot of flexibility. You can make it a 75 with gin, or try just champagne or sparkling wine with the Elderflower and Lemon Simple Syrup.

Serve this cocktail with Oysters on the Half Shell (page 45) and the Sakura Cherry Blossom Mignonette (page 46).

In a shaker, blend the gin and simple syrup with ice until chilled.

Strain into champagne flutes.

Top with the sparkling wine and rub a lemon twist on the rim, then garnish with the lemon twist and serve.

ROSES

There are thirty thousand species of cultivated roses and over 150 kinds of wild roses. For cooking with roses, I choose the ones with the most fragrance. As for foraging, the wild rose commonly found from Northern California to Alaska is the Nootka rose (*Rosa nutkana*). The flowers are small and super fragrant, and the stems lack thorns for the most part. They won't win any prizes in a flower show or become a metaphor in a poem about love, but they are great for foraging.

The other rose I like for foraging is the rugosa rose (*R. rugosa*). This one is not native but has gone feral, particularly in sandy coastal areas with full sun. These have the biggest, most flavorful rose hips.

And the third one I like to use is from my container garden. It's small, pink, super fragrant, and I have no idea what kind of rose it is. But it's easy foraging and I know there are no chemicals in that dirt.

Rose Hips

Rose hips are the seed-bearing fruit of a rose flower. They're beautiful in their own right, as shiny red beads that appear in the fall. They are all over the place and so very easy to forage. In colder climates, it's said to pick them after the first frost as that will sweeten the flavor. It doesn't usually frost where I live, so I wait until there's a few chilly snaps and then pick them. When I lived in Alaska, we'd string rose hips on dental floss and hang these garlands to dry in our cabins with wood-burning stoves. In Northern California, I dry them on baking sheets in the sun, or on very low temperatures in the oven. If you have a dehydrator, this works better than an oven. Though I prefer to use fresh rose hips, and *Rosa rugosa* have the largest hips and they are easier to clean the seeds from.

DIY: Rose Petal Honey

**MAKES ABOUT
2 CUPS**

**2 cups loosely packed
dried rose petals
(see note)**

**About 1 pound local
honey**

**Note: Rose petals and
buds are available
online or at stores that
sell bulk dried tea.**

Virtually all roses are safe to eat; just make sure they're organically grown or pesticide-free. Choose them based on their scent—the more fragrant the rose, the more strongly it will infuse the honey. After you pick the petals, wash and then set them out to dry. Using dried petals will keep the honey from getting watery. You can store dried rose petals and buds for up to a year before they start to fade. Use this honey on yogurt and scones, or as a condiment for cheese plates.

———————————————————

In a clean 16-ounce glass jar, add the rose petals. Pour the honey over the rose petals and cover with a lid.

Allow the honey to infuse for 2 weeks in a cupboard, turning the mixture every 5 days (as the petals tend to float to the top).

Strain out the petals in a colander, mashing the roses with a wooden spoon to wring out more honey. (Or you can leave them in—they can get messy and will continue infusing. If infusing for a long time, the flavor goes from floral to almost cinnamon-like.)

Pour the infused honey back into the jar. It will keep indefinitely, but after about a year may start to crystallize.

Rose Petal Honey Pots de Crème

MAKES 4 SERVINGS

4 large egg yolks

Pinch of kosher salt

⅓ cup Rose Petal Honey (page 253)

1 vanilla bean, split lengthwise

1½ cups heavy cream

½ cup whole milk

This is a recipe you make for your favorite people. It's not complicated and packs a lot of "wow." The honey is heated to almost burned and so has a dulce-de-leche taste to it. Extra credit if you infuse the cream with the vanilla bean overnight, but it's not necessary. The floral notes of rose are unexpected and have an almost cinnamon-spiced hint to the flavor. You can add a crunchy topping over it or dried rose petals for texture.

_____

Preheat the oven to 325 degrees F.

In a medium bowl, whisk the egg yolks and salt and set aside.

In a medium saucepan over medium-high heat, cook the honey, stirring occasionally, until it darkens and begins to bubble. You want a slightly overcooked smell, like dulce de leche. Scrape the vanilla bean into the honey.

Gradually add the cream and milk to the caramelized honey, stirring constantly.

Temper the egg yolks by adding a cup of the honey-cream mixture and whisking. Stream in the rest of the honey-cream mixture, whisking constantly.

Place ramekins in a large baking dish, and pour in boiling water around them so it comes halfway up the sides. Divide the custard mixture among the ramekins. Bake about 1½ hours, or until the edges of the custards are set but the centers still jiggle slightly.

Remove the ramekins from the water bath, and let the custards cool. Chill until firm, at least 2 hours.

Rose Hip and Apple Jam

**MAKES 4 CUPS OR
TWO 16-OUNCE JARS**

2 medium-firm tart-
sweet apples, finely
diced (about 2 cups)

2 cups water

1 cup rose hips, clean
and deseeded

1 tablespoon fresh
lemon juice

½ cup turbinado sugar

1 tablespoon tapioca
pearls

½ teaspoon ground
ginger

¼ teaspoon ground
allspice

¼ teaspoon ground
cinnamon

The best roses to scout for their fruit are *Rosa rugosa*, an introduced species from China that has taken off along the West Coast. The seedpods are big and flavorful and best after the first frost. But you can also try just regular rose hips as well. Use the apples you can forage, but if you buy them, I like to use Pink Lady or an apple that's both tart and semisweet and also has firm flesh. I don't bother to peel them, but you can if you like. The jam is great for thumbprint cookies, as filling for jelly donuts, layered into a linzer torte, or served with sharp cheddar cheese in an autumn charcuterie platter.

_____

In a medium saucepan over low heat, add the apples, water, rose hips, and lemon juice. Stir in the sugar, tapioca, and spices.

Simmer, stirring occasionally, for about 30 minutes. The mixture should thicken and the apples should be cooked all the way through. They'll look slightly translucent and soft.

In a blender or using an immersion blender, pulse the mixture a few times. I like it blended but still chunky, so don't puree it thoroughly. Also, if you're putting something warm in a blender, it may want to shoot out the top, so I recommend the immersion blender.

Return the mixture to the saucepan on low heat. Taste and adjust the spices as you like.

Ladle into two 16–ounce jars and refrigerate.

Use for the next week or so, or give the jars a warm water bath to seal them for longer-term storage.

Speckled Radicchio Winter Salad with Rose Hip and Orange Vinaigrette

MAKES 4 SERVINGS

1 small head of radicchio, cut into bite-size pieces

2 cups red butter lettuce, cut into 2–inch pieces

1 cup watercress, cut into 2–inch pieces

1 fennel bulb, thinly shaved with a mandoline

½ cup finely minced Pickled Cipollini Onions with Kumquats and Rose Hips (page 259) or shallots

¼ cup Rose Hip and Orange Vinaigrette (recipe follows)

Flaky sea salt, for finishing

1 avocado, ripe but firm, thinly sliced

1 Cara Cara orange, peeled, pithed, and cubed

¼ cup toasted, chopped walnuts

This winter salad layers the flavors of rosehip and orange both in the pickled onions and the vinegar for the dressing. These brighten and sweeten the bitterness of the chicory. The pickled onion adds sparks of flavor to the salad.

———————————————

In a large bowl, add the radicchio, butter lettuce, watercress, fennel, and pickled onions and toss with the dressing and finishing salt.

Plate the salad and top with the sliced avocado, orange pieces, and toasted walnuts and serve.

ROSE HIP AND ORANGE VINAIGRETTE

¾ cup extra-virgin
olive oil

¼ cup Rose Hip and
Orange–Infused
White Balsamic Vine-
gar (recipe follows) or
store-bought white
balsamic vinegar

Juice of 1 orange

1 teaspoon kosher salt

½ teaspoon white
pepper

This vinaigrette has a citrusy, effervescent flavor. It goes well with salads containing bitter greens. I also like to dress Dungeness crab, avocado, and citrus salad with it.

_____

In a small bowl, whisk all the ingredients together. Enjoy!

Rose Hip and Orange–Infused White Balsamic Vinegar

MAKES SLIGHTLY
OVER 2 CUPS

2 cups white balsamic
vinegar

Peels of 1 medium
navel orange

5 large rose hips from
rugosa roses, or 10
from smaller rose
plants

This vinegar works well as a dressing, to finished roasted vegetables, drizzled over fish, or even made into a shrub with winter citrus.

_____

In a 16-ounce jar with a lid, add all the ingredients and let the vinegar infuse for about a week. Keeps indefinitely.

Pickled Cipollini Onions with Kumquats and Rose Hips

**MAKES ONE 32-
OUNCE OR TWO 16-
OUNCE WIDE-MOUTH
MASON JARS**

2 cups white wine
   vinegar

2 cups water

2 tablespoons kosher
   salt

2 tablespoons sugar

17 to 20 cipollini or
   other small onions
   (about 4 cups)

10 whole kumquats

10 whole rugosa rose
   hips, washed and
   destemmed

Pickled onions are a staple for me. The kumquats and rose hips gild the lily. Use all three in a simple salad with avocado and some toasted nuts. Put them on pork tacos, braised white beans, a salmon fillet, or anything that could use some brightness and acid.

Peeling the onions is boring and tear-jerking, so I put on my snorkeling mask and listen to the *Ologies* or *Accidental Gods* podcasts while I'm doing it.

In a small saucepan over medium heat, add the vinegar, water, salt, and sugar and cook until the sugar and salt dissolve. Then let cool.

Slice the ends off each onion and peel the outer skins off.

Fill the mason jars with the onions, kumquats, and rose hips, alternating as you go.

Pour the pickling liquid to the top of the jars and store in the fridge.

They can be ready to use in just a few hours, or will last for about 4 weeks.

DIY: Floral Bitters

MAKES ABOUT 1 CUP

1½ cups Everclear grain
   alcohol or high-proof
   vodka

2 tablespoons dried
   rose petals

2 tablespoons dried
   lavender buds

2 tablespoons dried
   chamomile flowers

2 tablespoons dried
   elderflower

2 dried rose hips, or 1
   teaspoon rose hip
   powder

1 teaspoon fresh or
   dried dandelion root

Rose hips have a sultrier side; rather than a light, delicate floral flavor, they are bitter and make for a deeper and more complex addition to cocktails and mocktails. You can always substitute other edible flowers here. Just make sure you get some bitter ingredients in as well.

———————————————

In a 16-ounce jar, add all the ingredients, put on the lid, and shake. Store for a month in a dry, cool place. After a month, strain and bottle the liquid. (If you want the flavor more intense, just infuse it longer.)

CHERRY BLOSSOMS

Oh, what the springtime does to cherry trees, to paraphrase Pablo Neruda. These delightful taffy-pink blossoms put on a show, but there's no fruit forthcoming in these ornamentals. Still, pickled cherry blossoms are their own kind of springtime kismet. In Japan these blossoms are referred to as "sakura," and their appearance in the spring is a national holiday celebrated with lots of festivals and picnicking under the trees.

Preserved Sakura Cherry Blossom Truffles

MAKES 20 TO 25 TRUFFLES

⅔ cup heavy cream

8 ounces semisweet dark chocolate

1 teaspoon vanilla extract

2 tablespoons Preserved Sakura Cherry Blossoms (recipe follows) or dried rose petals or lavender, chopped

Truffles are super simple to make, delicious, and fun to let loose your creative impulses on. Roll them in ground bay laurel nuts (page 170), rose petals, a pinch of seaweed salt, or the most unexpected: top with sakura cherry blossoms.

Line a shallow pan with parchment paper.

In a small saucepan on medium-low heat, warm the cream.

In a mixing bowl, break up the chocolate into small chunks.

When the cream is warm, pour it over the chocolate. Add the vanilla. Count to fifty and stir the chocolate until it all melts.

Pour it into the pan, and when it cools, set in the fridge for 2 hours, or overnight so it firms up.

Remove from the fridge and let it come to room temperature.

Use a melon baller to scoop out the truffles. Store them in the fridge for up to a week (or the freezer for up to 3 months) until you are ready to serve them.

Sprinkle on a pinch of dried flowers just before serving. You don't need many of the blossoms to add a lot of flavor. Once they have the sakura on them, they won't store well.

MAKES 2 CUPS

10 cups cherry blos-
    soms with some
    leaves (3 blossoms to
    1 leaf), rinsed

1 cup kosher salt

1 cup ume plum vinegar

1 cup rice vinegar

PRESERVED SAKURA CHERRY BLOSSOMS

There's a Japanese tradition of preserving cherry blossoms in salt and ume plum vinegar, and then using the blossoms for tea or mixed with rice. They're also made into desserts for tea ceremonies. Preserved cherry blossoms are very salty, tart, and bracing, but also have a unique floral and fruity essence. I chop them into little pieces and sprinkle them onto ice cream with extra-virgin olive oil and flaky sea salt.

In a large bowl, add the blossoms and leaves and cover them with the salt. Lightly toss the flowers and leaves with the salt so everything is coated.

Add water until everything is submerged.

Cover them with a plate to hold the flowers down in the brine.

After 3 days, very gently strain out the water and toss the leaves. They are just there for added fragrance. Then pack the petals into a jar and fill with the ume plum and rice vinegar.

After 3 days in the vinegar, set your flowers out to dry or put on a baking sheet with a grate and set in the oven at the lowest-possible temperature.

When they are all dry, pack them into a jar and store in a cool, dry place. They will last at least a year, and start to discolor a bit after that.

I save the vinegar for other uses, sometimes adding a bit to the Sakura Cherry Blossom Mignonette (page 46).

Sakura Cherry Lemonade

MAKES 2 DRINKS

2 cups water

1 cup sugar

3 tablespoons fresh
lemon juice, divided

1 tablespoon chopped
Preserved Sakura
Cherry Blossoms
(page 264)

1 cup sparkling water

2 dashes Floral Bitters
(page 260) or Angos-
tura bitters

I passed along a jar of preserved cherry blossoms to my friend
Emile, without warning him what would happen if he just popped
one in his mouth. Apparently, the bracing effect stayed with him all
night. But then he came up with this tart, refreshing drink that also
makes a great cocktail.

———————————————

Bring the water to a boil and add the sugar. Simmer on low and stir,
dissolving the sugar.

Remove from the heat.

Stir 2 tablespoons of the lemon juice and the cherry blossoms into the
simple syrup.

When everything cools, mix 2 tablespoons of the simple syrup with the
remaining 1 tablespoon lemon juice, the sparkling water, and bitters and
mix. Divide between two glasses

VARIATION: MAKE IT A COCKTAIL

———————————————

Make the lemonade recipe as written, but add 3 ounces of vodka, such
as Ebb & Flow or Spirit Works, or Aviation American gin.

FIREWEED

Chamerion angustifolium

In Homer, Alaska, fireweed has a paradoxical beauty to it; whole undulated fields and exposed slopes are covered in the magnificent head-high purple-pink blooms that can reach nine feet in height. It's breathtaking—a pure Alice in Wonderland experience entering these thickets of beauty and foraging for it—but as the blooms of the flower all open, so goes the long-awaited summertime. By mid to late August, they are almost bloomed, and that means the winter chill is just around the corner.

Fireweed got its name from being one of the first plants to colonize burned ground after a volcano eruption or fire. It's abundant in Alaska and British Columbia, and found in most mountain ranges in the West. The color is particularly outstanding, the flavor mild in comparison—sort of floral tea with a hint of citrus and grass. Fireweed jellies and simple syrups are favorites to show off the color and flavor. The flowers and leaves can also be used for tea, and when young the shoots are said to have an asparagus-like flavor.

Fireweed Martini

MAKES 1 COCKTAIL

2 ounces gin

1 ounce Fireweed
Simple Syrup (recipe
follows)

1 dash Rum and Sea-
weed Bitters (page 27)
or Angostura bitters

Ice

Lemon twist, for garnish

These drinks are a showstopper, color-wise. With hints of floral and
seaweed and rum notes, they taste and look like coastal Alaska in
early August.

In a cocktail mixer or large glass jar, combine the gin, simple syrup, and
bitters with ice.

Shake and strain into a martini glass, then garnish with the lemon twist.

*MAKES ABOUT
2¼ CUPS*

3 cups fireweed blos-
soms, rinsed

3 cups water

1½ cups sugar

FIREWEED SIMPLE SYRUP

This is a great way to preserve fireweed blossoms, and the syrup can
be used throughout the rest of the year in cocktails and mocktails,
granitas, and sorbets.

In a large saucepan over medium heat, combine all the ingredients. Boil
for 15 minutes—not too long or it will become bitter.

Remove from the heat and strain. It should be a beautiful deep-laven-
der color. Store in a bottle with a tight lid. Enjoy!

URBAN-FORAGED DESSERTS GRAZING BOARD

Preserved Sakura Cherry Blossom Truffles (page 263)

Candy Cap Mushroom Shortbread Cookies (page 149)

Triple cream cheese (store-bought) with Raspberry and Chamomile Jam (page 229) and Seaweed, Seed, Oat, and Nut Bread (page 13) topped with Blackberry and Elderflower Compote (page 230)

Rose Petal Honey Pots de Crème (page 254)

Wild Berry and Peony Pavlova (page 221)

Fresh wild berries

SEASONAL MENUS

A GOOD MENU SHOULD HAVE THE musicality of a poem—a texture and rhythm, with a uniting thread through it. Our brains crave familiarity and novelty at the same time. We want comfort but also to be excited. Dishes must be trustworthy yet creative.

A menu also tells a story: like a narrative, it has rising action that draws people in, a climax, and a denouement. When creating a menu, I always consider what story I am trying to tell.

Ultimately, we are all telling our own stories through food—of nature and nurture, where we came from, what we see and love, and in our most ambitious moments, we stretch out of our culinary comfort zones to who we want to be. If we believe the adage, "Every story is a love story," then each menu we create is a love story. For me, that means bridging wilderness and regenerative farms with the people I cook for. Wild foods are my love language.

Seasonal menus are great—they express what's going on at the local farmers' markets, and I love to see how mounds of persimmons or peaches get translated onto the plate. But foragers know that the transition times are the really interesting ones—where foods overlap, or some just appear, while others linger. So rather than creating menus around seasons designated by farmers, these menus are in the blurry spaces between seasons, the very exciting times for foragers.

LATE WINTER TO EARLY SPRING

Sakura Cherry Lemonade (page 266)

Oysters on the Half Shell (page 45) with Sakura Cherry Blossom Mignonette (page 46)

Campfire Black Trumpet Flatbread with Pine Tips and Feta (page 123)

Miner's Lettuce, Pea Shoot, and Pickled Herring Salad (page 196)

Spaghetti with Herring Bottarga, Orange Zest, Ricotta, and Fresh Herbs (page 69)

Wild Trifle with Candy Cap Whipped Cream (page 145)

LATE SPRING TO SUMMER

Douglas Fir G & T (page 169)

Seaweed, Seed, Oat, and Nut Bread (page 13) with Seaweed Butter from Scratch (page 28) and Lemony Salt-Preserved Anchovies (page 80)

Seaweed and Citrus Salad with Mulberry-Kombu Vinaigrette (page 23)

Fire-Roasted Butter Clams with Seaweed Gremolata (page 36)

Wild King Salmon Bellies with Roasted Morels and Peaches (page 134)

Rose Petal Honey Pots de Crème (page 254)

FALL TO WINTER*

Blackberry del Bosque Mocktail (page 231)

Grilled Porcini on Rosemary Skewers with Porcini Butter (page 106)

Wild Green Savory Galette (page 198)

Speckled Radicchio Winter Salad with Rose Hip and Orange Vinaigrette (page 257)

Dungeness Crab Boil (page 52)

Grandma Mabe's Rum Pot Cake (page 241)
Bonus: This menu can be foraged entirely in urban spaces!

CAMPFIRE BRUNCH

Elderflower French 75 (page 250)

Pine Scones with Huckleberries (page 158)

Herby Mushroom Leek Toasts (page 99)

Spruce Tip and Juniper Berry Sockeye Salmon Gravlax (page 165) on bagels and cream cheese

Campfire Dashi-Poached Eggs with Vegetable Hash (page 17)

Flaming Pine Needle Mussels (page 43)

Bay Laurel Nut Hot Cocoa (page 173)

Chilled Huckleberries with Campfire Caramel and Seaweed Salt (page 225)

ACKNOWLEDGMENTS

THIS BOOK WOULD NOT EXIST WITHOUT Leslie Jonath's initial enthusiasm and encouragement. She and agent Leslie Stoker found it the perfect home with editor Jill Saginario at Sasquatch. Jill has been not only a great editor but enthusiastic about getting out and foraging. As well, photographer Marla Aufmuth is a passionate wildcrafter and her input has enriched the book. Anna Goldstein, art director at Sasquatch, has also been incredibly helpful and formative in the process of making this book. So many friends and neighbors have helped with giving feedback and recipe testing, along with accompanying me on foraging forays that sometimes don't go as planned; I can't name them all here, but thank you, village, in particular Emile Kfouri, who showed up at the final hour and helped create many of the cocktail recipes from a jumble of unfamiliar ingredients. I've also had many mentors who taught me about wild foods. Kevin Sadlier, who cofounded the Mycological Society of Marin, has shared his mushroom obsession with me and many others, and Heidi Herrman of Strong Arm Farm imparted her strong ethics around harvesting seaweed to me. I'd also like to thank Riley Starks of Nettles Farm on Lummi Island and Alison O'Hara in Homer, Alaska; both have been great collaborators for wild food camps, where a good portion of this book was photographed. I'd particularly like to thank my late grandmother, Vivian Stevermer, who taught me how to find feral asparagus in the spring and let me loose in her raspberry patch in late summer. She also taught me that there's always beauty—you just need to step outside and look up at the birds or down at the flowers.

INDEX

Note: Page numbers in *italic* refer to photographs.

Printed in China

SASQUATCH BOOKS with colophon is a registered trademark
of Penguin Random House LLC

28 27 26 25 24   9 8 7 6 5 4 3 2 1

Editor: Jill Saginario
Production editor: Peggy Gannon
Photographs: Marla Aufmuth
Designer: Anna Goldstein

Library of Congress Cataloging-in-Publication Data
Names: Finn, Maria, author. | Aufmuth, Marla, photographer.
Title: Forage. Gather. Feast. : recipes from West Coast forests, shores,
    and urban spaces / by Maria Finn ; photography by Marla Aufmuth.
Description: Seattle, WA : Sasquatch Books, [2024] | Includes index.
Identifiers: LCCN 2023022099 (print) | LCCN 2023022100 (ebook) |
    ISBN 9781632174864 (paperback) | ISBN 9781632174871 (epub)
Subjects: LCSH: Cooking (Wild foods) | Wild plants, Edible–Harvesting–
    Northwest, Pacific. | LCGFT: Cookbooks.
Classification: LCC TX823 .F438 2024 (print) | LCC TX823 (ebook) |
    DDC 641.6--dc23/eng/20230515
LC record available at https://lccn.loc.gov/2023022099
LC ebook record available at https://lccn.loc.gov/2023022100

The recipes contained in this book have been created for the
ingredients and techniques indicated. Neither publisher nor author is
responsible for your specific health or allergy needs that may require
supervision. Nor are publisher and author responsible for any adverse
reactions you may have to the recipes contained in the book, whether
you follow them as written or modify them to suit your personal dietary
needs or tastes.

ISBN: 978-1-63217-486-4

Sasquatch Books
1325 Fourth Avenue, Suite 1025
Seattle, WA 98101

SasquatchBooks.com

MIX
Paper | Supporting
responsible forestry
FSC® C008047